Please return/renew this item by the last date shown
on this label, or on your self-service receipt.

To renew this item, visit **www.librarieswest.org.uk**
or contact your library

Your borrower number and PIN are required.

LibrariesWest

Recreational Vehicles

A World History 1872–1939

Recreational Vehicles

A World History 1872–1939

ANDREW WOODMANSEY

MICHAEL SEDGWICK
MEMORIAL TRUST

Recreational Vehicles: A World History 1872-1939 is published with the financial assistance of the Michael Sedgwick Memorial Trust. The M.S.M.T. was founded in memory of the motoring historian and author Michael C. Sedgwick (1926–1983) to encourage the publication of new motoring research, and the recording of Road Transport History. Support by the Trust does not imply any involvement in the editorial process, which remains the responsibility of the editor and publisher. The Trust is a Registered Charity, No 290841, and a full list of the Trustees and an overview of the functions of the M.S.M.T. can be found on: www.michaelsedgwicktrust.co.uk

PEN & SWORD
TRANSPORT

AN IMPRINT OF PEN & SWORD BOOKS LTD.
YORKSHIRE – PHILADELPHIA

First published in Great Britain in 2022 by
Pen & Sword Transport
An imprint of Pen & Sword Books Ltd
Yorkshire - Philadelphia

ISBN 978 1 52679 245 7

Typeset in Palatino by SJmagic DESIGN SERVICES, India.
Printed and bound in India by Replika Press Pvt. Ltd.

Pen & Sword Books Ltd incorporates the Imprints of Pen & Sword Books Archaeology, Atlas, Aviation, Battleground, Discovery, Family History, History, Maritime, Military, Naval, Politics, Railways, Select, Transport, True Crime, Fiction, Frontline Books, Leo Cooper, Praetorian Press, Seaforth Publishing, Wharncliffe and White Owl.

For a complete list of Pen & Sword titles please contact:

PEN & SWORD BOOKS LIMITED
47 Church Street, Barnsley, South Yorkshire, S70 2AS, England
E-mail: enquiries@pen-and-sword.co.uk
Website: www.pen-and-sword.co.uk

Or

PEN AND SWORD BOOKS
1950 Lawrence Rd, Havertown, PA 19083, USA
E-mail: Uspen-and-sword@casematepublishers.com
Website: www.penandswordbooks.com

Half title page image: Noel Pemberton Billing's Road Yacht (UK, 1927)

Title page image: A contemporary sketch of the *Grande Diligence* of Prince Oldenburg (France, 1896)

Image captions include location and year of the image in brackets (where known).

CONTENTS

PREFACE

The term 'recreational vehicle' is a relatively modern one. It was in use in America by 1940, but it neatly captures a family of vehicles that began to appear on the roads of Europe and America over 130 years ago. Definitions of a recreational vehicle vary, so for clarity this book defines a recreational vehicle, or 'RV' for short, as a road vehicle that contains sleeping facilities and is used for leisure. Today's RVs include caravans ('travel trailers' in the USA), motorhomes, camper trailers, teardrops, fifth wheelers and many others. All are the descendants of a small number of horse-drawn RVs dating back to the late 1800s. There is no distinction made in this history between today's two major RV categories, the caravan and the motorhome, since each is an RV, distinguished only by the presence or absence of an engine. The shifting preferences between the two over time is part of RV history. This book focuses on the important formative years of RV development in several countries from 1872 until the start of the Second World War.

Recreational Vehicles: A World History 1872-1939 has been written for three main reasons. Firstly, evidence of the early history of the RV is disparate and fragmented. The stories of the RV pioneers are fading along with the memories of their descendants, suggesting that early RV history needs to be captured whilst there is still time. Thanks to the untiring efforts of digital archivists in the last decade or so, pieces of the RV jigsaw puzzle have been preserved and await assembly by the patient historian. The research for this book has revealed hitherto unknown RVs from the late 1800s and early 1900s – some early RV photographs or engravings are reproduced here in print for the first time.

Secondly, an international history of the RV has to the author's knowledge never previously been published. This book features a selection of early RVs from the six main countries that have adopted the RV: the UK, France, USA, Germany, Australia and New Zealand. Early French and German RVs are described in English probably for the first time, re-balancing the Anglocentric coverage of RV history to date. An international approach to RV history allows an illuminating comparison between RVs of different countries, highlighting differences but also similarities in vehicle design and leisure cultures.

Thirdly, early RVs are better understood if seen in their original context. By featuring only period black and white photographs, each RV can be seen in its own place and time. Many photographs feature proud builders, owners or hirers, offering a glimpse into the scenes, fashions and customs of the time and an insight into a less-explored part of our leisure history.

The book is not an RV catalogue or an index of RV manufacturers. Instead, it is a curated selection of early RVs from countries where these vehicles have become part of the leisure culture. Each RV illustrates a significant milestone in the development of RV use, design or engineering. Some special purpose coaches, caravans and motorhomes are featured in the final chapter, showing how these machines have been adapted to purposes beyond leisure.

Semi-permanent 'mobile homes' are not included, since they are generally used as low-cost housing and thus not recreational in the sense used here. Similarly, gypsy caravans are included only as a design and lifestyle reference for early British caravanners, since they too were not recreational. The development and use of dedicated RV parks is not discussed. Regretfully, due to space constraints or scarcity of historical records, some countries with a known history of early RV manufacturing and use such as the Netherlands, Denmark, Italy and Canada have not been included.

Source material comes from national, regional and local libraries around the world as well as the archives of motoring and RV organisations. Private collectors of RV publications and memorabilia have made an invaluable contribution to this history. Records are being updated continuously, so it is a certainty that further details of early RVs will come to light in the years ahead. This is to be welcomed, since new discoveries will further enrich the history of the RV.

It is hoped that the international, curated and contextual approach of this book will widen its appeal beyond a specialist RV audience to anyone interested in transport and leisure history.

Advertising for Eccles caravans (UK, c1926)

INTRODUCTION

The RV is an enigma. In some countries it is unheard of, but in others it is highly popular. Reaction to the RV ranges from bemusement to enchantment, from wariness to pride. In the six main countries covered by this book, there are today estimated to be about 15 million RVs, of which about 10 million are in the USA. They come in all shapes and sizes and are used by families, couples, singles, millionaires, workers, 'grey nomads' and members of the 'van life' and 'tiny house' movements. Those that own an RV today see it as an affordable, low impact, self-contained and healthy way to enjoy a holiday. So, what is the appeal of the RV and why do we need to know about its history?

On a practical level the RV offers the traveller the opportunity to experience the outdoor life in home-like levels of comfort. On a broader level it offers freedom. Freedom from the schedules of trains, planes and ships, freedom to explore new places whilst sleeping somewhere familiar, freedom to abandon urban existence and reconnect with nature. The RV is a small house on wheels that allows its occupants to vary at will their surroundings, their schedules and their companions.

Just as the RV itself is a quirky combination of propulsion, accommodation and a few creature comforts, so the history of the RV is a blend of our social, leisure and transport past. RVs would not have come about without good roads, beautiful places to visit and the time and money for recreation. RVs thrived when travel changed from being a means to an end to an end in itself. So a book that simply catalogued a list of early RVs might interest some, but would not explain why these vehicles were developed.

Those who feel today that an RV holiday is good for body and soul, for example, might be interested to know that some of the earliest RV users were American 'health seekers' escaping the east coast tuberculosis epidemics of the nineteenth century. Those wishing to escape the daily grind of modern city life by returning to nomadic ways might find equivalent sentiments among the 'gentlemen gypsies' of late nineteenth-century Britain. And those who yearn for an outdoor holiday in greater luxury than that offered by a tent may find vindication of their wishes in the large number of RV manufacturers who started business with exactly that motivation.

Contrary to popular belief, the history of the RV begins well before the advent of the internal combustion engine. The first RVs were horse-drawn, emerging when vehicles designed for other uses were adapted for leisure in late nineteenth-century Britain. RVs were not invented but evolved over time from a broad range of other horse-drawn vehicles including stage wagons, circus caravans, gypsy *vardos*, living wagons and even bathing machines. The motorized RV era opened with the French steam-powered RVs of the 1890s followed by the more widespread petrol driven, truck-based motorhomes of the early 1900s. Both were a far cry from the luxury, streamlined caravans and travel trailers that eventually appeared just before the Second World War.

An international perspective sheds new light on RV history. The pre-eminence of the UK and the USA in RV design and manufacturing is well known, but less well known are the important RV design contributions of other countries such as France, with its lightweight RVs of the 1920s, and Germany, with its folding camper trailers and lightweight caravans of the 1930s. On the other side of the world, Australia's good climate but poor road conditions created the environment for early 'pop-top'caravans with good ground clearance. New Zealand's narrow, winding and flood-prone roads led to advances in small, agile caravans and motorhomes.

During the research for this book, the history of the RV has been partially re-written. It is now clear that the RV is older than some may have thought. As yet undiscovered RVs may further change this understanding. The pre-1939 period is arguably the richest and most illuminating period in the development of the RV, from the early pioneers to the experimenters, from the aircraft designers to the lifestyle salesmen, from the self-built to the mass-produced and from boom to bust. RV builders and users of today may discover that there is very little that is new in the RV world, and that some RV designs around today are in fact over a hundred years old.

Those who have fallen for the RV have one thing in common: non-conformity. Throughout history designers, builders and users of the RV have thought and acted 'out of the box'. This collection of old RVs shows their bravery and ingenuity and appeals to the maverick in us all.

An Airstream Clipper (USA, 1936)

CHAPTER 1
RECREATIONAL VEHICLE ORIGINS AND INFLUENCES

" The rise of the caravan has, in proportion to its scale, the same hall marks as the rise of the railways and even the French Revolution or the English Industrial Revolution. **"**

from *The Caravan and its Impact on Society*
by W. M. Whiteman, 1957

The *maison ambulante* or travelling house of Melchior Bardier (Netherlands, 1751)

Dwellings on Wheels

Our yearning for a nomadic life has not come about by chance – today's RV users are just following their instincts. *Homo sapiens* has been around for about 200,000 years, but most of our race decided to settle in one place only around 12,000 years ago. Nomads would travel seasonally or year-round to find food and new pastures for their animals, but from about 10,000 BCE humans began to farm in one place and build static communities. So with around ninety-five per cent of our history being nomadic, it's no surprise that we still retain some of our travelling genes.

The earliest dwellings on wheels took the form of portable shelters drawn by animals. The nomadic tribes of the Eurasian steppes such as the Sarmatians and the Scythians were likely to have been the first users of wheeled shelters. Toys excavated from Kerch, in what is now east Crimea, date back to about 600 BCE and show what are probably portable shelters made by the Sarmatians. These were built on wooden boards or poles that would be lifted from carts to the ground at the end of a day's travel.

Wheeled vehicles were in use in many parts of Europe by the third millennium BCE. The Egyptians and the Greeks were known for developing the simple cart into the wagon and the chariot, but it was the Romans who advanced both roads and road transport in leaps and bounds. We have good records of at least fifteen different types of Roman carts and wagons that were used to equip the Roman army and supply its citizens along the vast Roman road network. One of these was the *carruca,* a four-wheeled carriage designed for extended travel. In the later years of the Roman Empire there are references to a derivative of this type of carriage called the *carruca dormitoria* or 'sleeping carriage'. It included a basic bed for use on longer journeys. Wheels were generally wooden, but more sophisticated versions had metal-rimmed wheels. The Romans can be credited with a number of other engineering firsts in the wagon field including rim brakes, basic suspension and even a primitive odometer consisting of stones rotating in wooden-toothed barrels. Pivoting front axles were used by the Romans in their wagons but were probably invented by the Gauls.

The Anglo Saxons who inhabited Britain from the fifth to the eleventh centuries were less mobile than the Romans but would still move between towns to trade and hold fairs. Most travel would have been on horseback, but an engraving of a tenth-century Anglo Saxon 'wheel bed', including the suspension of a hammock-style bed from posts (a technique which gave vehicle suspension its name), offers a hint of how simple wagons may have been adapted for sleeping on longer journeys in the Middle Ages.

The Mongols of Asia were true nomads, usually moving twice a year to new grazing grounds for their stock. They would take their pre-built, round tents or *gers* with them on wagons and position these on the ground at each new location. A legendary example was the *ger* of Genghis Khan which he

A Scythian house on wheels (Central Asia, c900-200 BCE)

An Anglo-Saxon *chaer* or wheel bed (UK, tenth century)

Genghis Khan's *ger* pulled by twenty-two oxen, as depicted in *The Travels of Marco Polo* (Asia, c1300)

used for accommodation whilst waging battle in the late twelfth century. It was reputedly pulled by twenty-two oxen and was kept under constant guard in camp.

Between the seventeenth and nineteenth centuries, a number of kings, queens and members of the aristocracy including Cardinal Richelieu, Napoleon and several European and Russian princes are known to have had luxurious horse-drawn coaches built for them to make long journeys more comfortable, but few of these had dedicated provisions for sleeping. Mobile, house-like structures built for purposes other than accommodation

began to appear in Europe in the eighteenth century. The *maison ambulante* or travelling house invented by Melchior Bardier of France in 1751 (see page 11) is a lesser-known example of how a collapsible display structure was built and transported in the eighteenth century. It is believed that this contraption may have been used as a form of travelling museum to display paintings and artefacts of French battles and early inventions. But it was another type of vehicle that arguably forms the strongest genetic link between the modern RV and its ancestors – the British seventeenth-century 'caravan'.

The First Caravans (1640)

The word 'caravan' provides a useful clue as to the early origins of the RV. 'Caravan' has two principal meanings in modern English usage. It is derived from the Persian word 'karwan', meaning a group of people travelling together through a dangerous place for safety. This leads to its first meaning – a form of convoy. In British English it has a second meaning, a mobile trailer incorporating accommodation, known today in the USA as a travel trailer. So where did this usage come from?

The use of the word 'caravan' to describe an *individual* vehicle rather than a group of people, camels or vehicles was first recorded in seventeenth-century Britain. The term was used colloquially in some parts of the country to describe a horse-drawn vehicle called a stage wagon or long wagon. These were slow, heavy wagons that transported goods and people between towns. They appeared in around 1640, a hundred years or so before their more elaborate and swifter cousin, the stagecoach.

According to Charles Harper's *Stage Coach and Mail in Days of Yore*, written in 1903:

'Travellers from the Far East had originally brought the word ('caravan') to England. They had seen the Persian 'karwans' toiling under those torrid skies – covered wagons in whose shady interiors the poor folk travelled; and when the first stage-waggons were established in England, they were often known by an English version of that name.'

It seems then that it was the nature of these wagons, in essence goods vehicles that also carried passengers, rather than how they travelled in convoy, which led such vehicles to be called 'caravans'. There was nowhere to sleep in these first British caravans – passengers slept at inns along the way. During the seventeenth and eighteenth centuries, public fee-paying caravan services were established between a number of British towns and cities. They were dark, slow and uncomfortable, leading to travel sickness among some passengers.

Luggage was invariably piled high on a caravan's flat roof, sometimes to such an extent that it would fall off en route and be stolen. Windows were a later addition and the stench of unwashed passengers in these early public caravans was often remarked upon in travellers' diaries. Caravans were used to convey prisoners from London to the hulk ships moored off Portsmouth and other British ports that housed convicts until their transportation to Australia between 1788 and 1868.

Although the quality, comfort and speed of public caravans improved modestly over time, they were always the second class cousins of the stagecoach. With the arrival of the railways

A stage wagon, also colloquially known as a 'caravan'. Laden with both goods and passengers, it needed wide wheels to reduce road damage (UK, 1820)

Caravan Powder (1755)

The *London Daily Advertiser* of 7 November 1755 advertised a treatment for the sickness caused by travelling in cramped, airless caravans. It was called 'caravan powder', which was described as:

'a commodious Aliment for passengers in the Eastern Caravans, and for all other People. It is a species of grocery, which they use in the same manner as Coffee, and the Liquor made of it is an elegant and comfortable Repast. It prevents Injuries from unwholesome Air, Damps, and Vapours, so fatal in their Effects, recruits their Strength and Spirits, and enables them to undergo their toilsome Journeys, and other Labours, with Cheerfulness.'

N.B. The reference to 'Eastern Caravans' is a likely reference to east London, the poorest and least healthy part of the city at the time.

An engraving titled 'The Caravan'. Horse-drawn caravan services needed to increase speed to compete with railways introduced in the 1830s (UK, 1838)

in Britain in about 1830, caravans quickly became third class. Some early third class railway carriages were called 'caravans', once again because they carried goods and people. As the railways expanded and railway carriage standards improved, passengers were separated from their heavy luggage, the latter being consigned to a 'luggage caravan' at the rear of a train. Over time this was abbreviated to 'luggage van' or 'goods van', terms still used to this day on the railways. The final stage of the evolution of the term 'caravan' in this sense was for its abbreviated form 'van' to become associated with any vehicle, whether on rail or road, carrying goods only.

Compared to railway travel in Britain in the mid-nineteenth century, lumbering horse-drawn caravan services soon became unattractive. They ran to faster timetables to try to compete with the railways, but to no avail. Most such services ended, and as they did so, many public caravans were sold off to private owners. Buyers included travelling circuses and menageries, later followed by gypsies and tinkers. Most would convert their caravan into mobile accommodation. For these groups, the large size of a caravan was an advantage, since they were big enough to live in when travelling, along with beds and other furniture.

When the first brave travellers of the late 1800s started to roam the British countryside in a horse-drawn vehicle for purely recreational purposes, there was therefore little doubt as to what it should be called. In recognition of the fact that it carried both goods and people, it was without doubt a caravan.

Entertainment in Caravans

The average citizen of Britain and Europe in the seventeenth and eighteenth centuries rarely travelled far from home. Farm workers had little need to travel, since farming families lived close together and everything they needed was nearby. Family members did not begin to travel more extensively until the impact of the Industrial Revolution became widespread in the early nineteenth century. For recreation, country dwellers attended local fairs and celebrations of patron saints called wakes. Any form of amusement had to be affordable and close to home. To meet this need, some entrepreneurial entertainers built or purchased caravans to show, transport and guard a range of attractions that ranged from the curious to the grotesque.

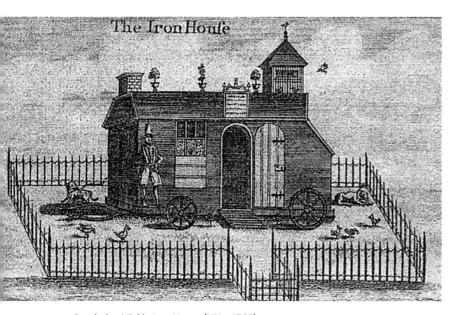

Batchelor Nick's *Iron House* (UK, c1765)

One example was the *Iron House* of 1765, owned by a certain 'Batchelor Nick'. This was a mobile curiosity placed outside pubs between Bath, Oxford and London. According to a flyer used to promote the *Iron House*, it was literally a house on wheels and contained a fireplace for roasting meat, a pigeon loft, bird cages, a collection of arms, a bed and two cellars. Its walls were covered with paintings of famous battles and stately homes and 'Sir Isaac Newton's Optical' (possibly a glass prism). The house was guarded by a 'grenadier' and surrounded by a 'very curious new fashioned pallisade'. Batchelor Nick had clearly seen an opportunity to make money from local pub patrons by charging them to view a motley collection of birds, objects and paintings.

The commercial display of people with unusual features or from far-off lands was a common 'entertainment' of the late eighteenth and early nineteenth centuries. In 1811, for example, visitors to Hull's marketplace were given the opportunity to view 'in a commodious caravan' the unfortunate Mrs Weston, described as 'a dwarf who was six inches shorter than any woman travelling'. Accompanying Mrs Weston was another 'Liliputian Dwarf' and a model of the Grand Turk's Palace in Constantinople. Admission to the caravan was one shilling for 'Ladies and Gentlemen', sixpence for 'Trades People' and threepence for children. Attraction owners and even the attractions themselves would sleep in their display caravans as they travelled between towns.

Circuses and Menageries

The first private owners of caravans on any scale were European menagerie owners and travelling circuses. From the late 1700s until the early twentieth century, lions, tigers, elephants and other exotic animals were caught alive in their native countries and brought to Europe by explorers and hunters. They were acquired by entrepreneurs and taken on tours of cities and towns in wheeled cages for display to an amazed and sometimes fearful fee-paying public. British newspapers of the mid-1800s were full of articles reporting the escape of lions, bears and snakes from their cages, causing havoc in the local community. Menagerie owners would travel and sleep in simple but comfortable mobile living quarters adapted from former public caravans or purpose-built by coachbuilders. Over time, menagerie caravans became more elaborate to attract the public's attention. Once the novelty of seeing these unusual beasts had worn off, the animals were taught to perform tricks. They became a feature of both

Manders Menagerie (UK, 1910)

Some of the first people to use accommodation on wheels included surveyors, photographers, writers, agricultural workers and road builders.

The private horse-drawn carriage called the *britzka*, also known in French as a *dormeuse*, was a long-distance travel coach that could be used for sleeping. Originating from Poland in the early nineteenth century, it had a box under the driver's seat that could accommodate the legs of sleeping passengers when the seats inside the carriage were laid flat. Isambard Kingdom Brunel travelled and slept in a *britzka* during his surveying work for the construction of the British Great Western Railway in 1833. The Duke of Beaufort also owned a *britzka*, preferring it to coaching inns during his travels. His *britzka* is now part of the collection of the Museum of Bristol.

As photography became more advanced in the mid-1800s, it became a new occupation for a few. Early professional photographers would sometimes travel long distances to capture images of remote places or events. Photographic equipment of the period was both cumbersome and fragile. Photographers needed flexible vehicles to carry their precious equipment and provide accommodation en route. Thus by chance photography became a catalyst for new forms of accommodation on wheels.

permanent and travelling circuses, leading to a decline in the popularity of the travelling menagerie.

The circus has been an important form of entertainment since Roman times – it was accessible, exciting and exotic. During the nineteenth century, static circuses were gradually replaced by travelling circuses that of necessity became significant caravan users. Circus caravans ranged in style from simple wagons for sleeping to elaborate promotional vehicles used in circus parades on arrival in town.

Working Caravans

Early caravan travel in Britain is often associated with the romance of horse-drawn gypsy wagons travelling along tree-lined country lanes. The reality of eighteenth- and nineteenth-century road travel in Britain was far more prosaic – it was often dangerous, uncomfortable and time-consuming. Dangerous because of the risk of highway robbery, uncomfortable because roads were largely dirt tracks and time-consuming because horses were slow. Travelling for leisure under such circumstances would have been unthinkable at the time. Such vehicles that ventured on the roads with sleeping facilities were used mainly for work.

The *britzka* or *dormeuse* of the Duke of Beaufort, with an extended front section for sleeping (UK, 1827)

Roger Fenton's assistant Marcus Sparling seated on Fenton's photographic van (UK, 1855)

Samuel White Baker and party at Larnaca (Cyprus, 1879)

Roger Fenton was one such travelling photographer who documented the Crimean War in 1855. He travelled with his assistant Marcus Sparling in a 'photographic van' which served as a mobile darkroom as well as accommodation. Fenton also carried a separate developing tent. The photographic process of the day required a large volume of delicate equipment including cameras, chemicals and glass plates. Fenton's van was converted from a former wine-merchant's van, so may have been well suited to carrying fragile items, but it was less successful as a bedroom and darkroom. When Fenton reached the Crimea, he found the heat and flies intolerable and the fumes of his developing chemicals proved on one occasion almost fatal.

Explorers were also early caravan users. One was Samuel White Baker. Sometimes described as the first caravan holiday, Baker's trip to Cyprus in 1879 was in fact a research trip. Baker was a hunter and explorer who in later life went to Cyprus to write a book about the island called *Cyprus As I Saw It*. Baker had two horse-drawn caravans shipped out from London, because, in his words, 'the miserable reports in England respecting the want of accommodation and the unhealthiness of Cyprus had determined me to render myself independent.'

A type of mobile accommodation called the 'living van' or 'sleeping van' was a popular form of workers' mobile accommodation in a number of countries in the late nineteenth and early twentieth centuries. The living van was used by agricultural and road workers and was usually towed by a traction engine. Steam tractors were in high demand for road building and agriculture and worked in pairs, so their owners would move them from job to job as fast as they could to increase revenue. To save time, traction engine owners took their workers with them, accommodating them in living vans. A living van was extremely basic, containing firm bunk beds, a stove and little else. In the early models of the 1870s and 1880s, ventilation was poor and suffocation was a high risk when the stove was lit. British living van manufacturers such as Fowlers and the Bristol Carriage Company created their own designs. The living vans of the late nineteenth century were thus the first ever road vans to be pulled by machine rather than animal. In their shape, size and materials used, glimpses of the first recreational vans can be seen.

A Fowler steam ploughing engine with living van, harrow and water cart for fully self-contained agricultural work (UK, c1900)

Other workers who used accommodation on wheels during the nineteenth century included tinkers, quacks, shepherds and missionaries. The latter were significant caravan users in a number of countries, preaching the gospel in remote areas and overseas. Some examples of so-called 'bible vans' can be seen in Chapter Eight.

The Gypsy Wagon

The gypsy wagon had a major influence on the first recreational vehicle users of Britain. Contrary to popular myth, gypsies were not the first to live in caravans. Circus and menagerie owners were doing so from the early 1800s onwards, whilst gypsies developed a caravan culture in Britain only after 1850. Prior to using caravans, gypsy communities such as the Romany of Europe were mainly tent dwellers, building 'bender' tents out of bent sapling branches covered in tarpaulin, blankets or felt. Later, gypsies would use caravans and tents side by side for many years.

The gypsy wagon or *vardo* evolved over time, beginning in the 1850s as a simple wagon and transforming late in the century into an ornately-carved caravan that became a status symbol for its owner. The richer the family, the more ornate their *vardo*. There were six main types, each carrying unique design features. The most sought after was the Reading, named after the location of its principal manufacturer, Dunton and Sons of Reading. Not only was it beautifully decorated, it was also highly practical, using large wheels to navigate poor roads and streams.

Inside, *vardos* would generally have a cast-iron cooking stove with chimney, seating, beds, cabinets, mirrors and a display cabinet for china. The entrance would be at the front, whilst lantern windows (slit windows built into the roof) were used in later models. In keeping with Romany tradition, most *vardos* would be burned along with other possessions on the death of the owner. Hence few early examples survive today. In the early twentieth century, the tradition of building highly elaborate *vardos* passed and gypsy caravans became more utilitarian.

A gypsy family and their *vardo* in Battersea, London (UK, 1877)

Throughout history gypsies have been subjected to discrimination and harassment. In the mid to late 1800s, resentment of gypsies among the general population was particularly strong. By contrast, the first users of recreational vehicles in Britain were supporters of the gypsy culture and lifestyle. Between 1885 and 1894 there were nine attempts to introduce an anti-gypsy Movable Dwellings Bill in Britain. These failed when non-gypsy showmen rallied against the

bill, but gypsy encampments would continue to be broken up or moved on well into the 1900s. But in the late 1800s, against popular sentiment, a few English gentlemen and ladies decided to emulate the Romanies' nomadic culture. The simple, outdoor life was seen as an antidote to the ills of the Industrial Revolution. In Britain, these people became known as 'gentlemen gypsies' and it is they who developed and used the first-ever recreational vehicles.

The Birth of Recreational Travel

A Grand Tour to Venice, Rome and other cultural capitals of Europe was an educational and cultural rite of passage for the young nobility of Britain in the seventeenth and eighteenth centuries. In the nineteenth century however, European wars forced the gentry to look closer to home for their educational tours. Inspired by the works of romantic painters and writers, the Victorian upper and middle classes would instead combine a visit to the British countryside or a spa town with a tour of a nearby stately home or natural feature. These tours were private, predominantly educational and highly structured – early Victorian travel guide writers would invariably tell their readers exactly where to stand to get the best views and what thoughts to have when looking at a particular scene. During the Romantic Movement of the nineteenth century, nature was recast from 'wild' to 'sublime'. Instead of something to be feared, natural beauty spots such as the English Lake District or the Scottish Highlands became destinations to be painted or written about by those wealthy enough to reach them by private transport.

The advent of the railways in the 1830s brought affordable travel to the masses for the first time. Often to the dismay of the British upper classes, the railways opened up new destinations hitherto reserved for the wealthy. One of the world's first travel agents, Thomas Cook, was quick to see the potential of affordable organized tours by rail, taking a paying group of around 500 teetotallers from Leicester to Loughborough in 1840. He was one of many to organize rail and accommodation excursions to London for the Great Exhibition of 1851. The exhibition gave millions of country people the opportunity to visit and tour London for the first time. Travel packages were arranged to include rail transport and accommodation, and thus large-scale commercial tourism was born.

There was, however, one problem that prevented working people from becoming tourists – a lack of free time. A six- or even seven-day working week was common for workers during

Visitors going to the Great Exhibition on 'Shilling Day' in Hyde Park, London (UK, 1851)

the Industrial Revolution, leaving little time for recreation. Paid holidays were unknown in most industrialized countries until the early twentieth century. In early Victorian Britain, there was neither the time nor the money for leisure unless wealth was inherited. Matters improved for workers in the late 1800s with the combination of local, national and bank holidays (the latter introduced in 1871) generating about two weeks unpaid holiday a year. Factory owners preferred these holidays to be taken at once to permit a full factory shutdown. For a brief period each year, then, workers were able to seek out new forms of affordable leisure at the beach, in the parks and on the sports fields of the country.

If increased time off work provided one incentive to take holidays, the poor quality of urban life provided another. The Industrial Revolution had brought sweeping social change, first to Britain and later America and parts of Europe. Factories and mines brought prosperity to their owners but often misery to their workers. The lives of those living in cities became dirtier, noisier and generally less healthy. A holiday was an opportunity to get fresh air and exercise.

Among the elite in Britain there were some who despaired at what they saw as the diminishing quality of life and the loss of traditional craftsmanship brought about by mass production. The Arts and Crafts movement was created in response to the

Ailments Likely to be Benefited by Caravan Life (1886)

The health benefits of recreational caravanning were identified at an early stage and contributed to the hobby's growth. Dr William Gordon Stables, the owner of *The Wanderer* caravan and a retired naval surgeon, had his own views on the subject, which he set out in a book describing his first long caravan journey in 1885. In listing the 'ailments likely to be benefited by caravan life' he wrote:

'I can, of course, only mention a few of these, and it must be distinctly understood that I am not trying to enforce the merits of a new cure. I am but giving my own impressions from my own experience, and if anyone likes to profit by these he may, and welcome.

    I.   Ennui.
    II.   Dyspepsia.
    III. Debility and enfeeblement of health from overwork, or from worry or grief.
    IV. Insomnia.
    V.   Chronic bronchitis and consumption in its earliest stages.
    VI. Bilious habit of system.
    VII. Acidity of secretions of stomach, etc.
  VIII. All kinds of stomachic ailments.
    IX. Giddiness or vertigo.
    X.   Hysteria.
    XI. Headaches and wearying backaches.
   XII. Constipated state of system.
  XIII. Tendency to embonpoint.
  XIV. Neuralgia of certain kinds.
   XV. Liver complaints of a chronic kind.
  XVI. Threatened kidney mischief.
 XVII. Hay fever.
XVIII. Failure of brain power.
  XIX. Anaemia or poverty of blood.
   XX. Nervousness.'

from *The Cruise of The Land Yacht "Wanderer" or Thirteen Hundred Miles in my Caravan* by Dr William Gordon Stables (1886)

industrialisation of England. Led by art critic John Ruskin and designer William Morris, the movement firmly believed that a healthy and moral person needed to make things by hand using designs inspired by nature. The first leisure caravan owners of Britain saw an opportunity to kill two birds with one stone. They believed that a return to a healthier lifestyle could be achieved by escaping from polluted, noisy cities into the countryside. Not only that, but following the principles of the Arts and Crafts movement, they would travel in caravans built by craftsmen.

The First Leisure Vehicles: Charabancs and Bathing Machines

Two distant relatives of the leisure caravan played an early role in popularising the use of vehicles for leisure purposes. One of the earliest forms of leisure vehicle was the horse-drawn *char à banc*. This carriage with benches was a French innovation from the early 1800s, used to take private groups to watch horse races or go on hunting trips. In 1844 Queen Victoria was presented with a *char à banc* by Louis-Philippe of France. The charabanc, as it came to be known in the UK, soon found favour among the well-to-do for short excursions. The motorized versions of charabancs would later become popular amongst the working classes in early twentieth-century Britain as they took workers on organized day excursions to the seaside, and more often than not, to the pub.

An even earlier leisure vehicle was the bathing machine. The health benefits of bathing in the sea were known and promoted by physicians from the mid-1700s. First developed in England in the 1750s to allow women to bathe in the sea unseen by men, bathing machines consisted of a wooden changing hut on wheels with a ladder covered by a fabric canopy at the rear. The canopy allowed (mainly) ladies to enter and exit the water in private. The machines were taken down to the water's edge by horse, and once in the water, women were not expected to swim beyond the canopy. Some machines used flags operated by the bather at the end of the swim to notify the machine operator on shore that she was suitably attired and ready to be retrieved from the water.

Bathing machines thrived in countries where sex segregation on beaches was practised. Segregated bathing ended in Britain in 1901 and the use of bathing machines declined rapidly thereafter. Some bathing machines were later turned into recreational caravans, whilst others became the first of the beach huts that are today seen lining many British beaches. Queen Victoria's bathing machine, used at her private beach on the Isle of Wight in southern England, remains part of the collection of her summer estate on the island, Osborne House.

Bathing machines at Coogee Beach, Sydney (Australia, c1880-1900)

The Birth of the RV

In late nineteenth-century Britain, then, conditions slowly developed for the emergence of a new pastime. Caravans first used to provide a basic form of public transport were sold off and converted to private mobile accommodation by a wide range of users. Workers lived in vans to save on accommodation costs and get more work done. For gypsies, the caravan became a way of life and served as a status symbol. Caravans of all shapes and sizes had become a familiar sight on British roads. At the same time, the recreational possibilities of vehicles had become apparent in two very different leisure activities – sightseeing and sea bathing.

With the backdrop of British industrialisation and rampant urbanisation, the emergence of the RV was spurred on by increased leisure time, a greater appreciation of nature and the pursuit of better health. Despite the risks, discomforts and practical shortcomings of living on the road, the road network was improving. So it was that a few wealthy but brave city-dwellers stopped dreaming of the nomadic life and took to their caravans. The gentlemen gypsies of Britain set off for the countryside in the first ever recreational vehicles.

CHAPTER 2

THE UNITED KINGDOM

"
To enjoy caravanning don't be taciturn. Be affable and agreeable, wear a smile on your face and talk freely to those who are similarly disposed, and you will never find the road dull.
"

from *Caravanning and Camping Out*
by J. Harris Stone (1914)

Opposite: Caravanners H. Owen Scott and his wife pictured with their pets at a pebble-bordered site at Lepe Shore in the New Forest. The caravan is from the hire fleet of Bertram Hutchings (UK, 1913)

The UK is rightly regarded as the home of the recreational caravan. The UK's rich history of multi-purpose caravan use from the early 1800s laid the groundwork for the introduction of recreational caravanning in the late 1800s. But the new hobby had to overcome a major hurdle before it gained greater acceptance by late Victorian society. Caravans and their occupants had an image problem.

The number of caravans on British roads and lanes grew steadily as the nineteenth century progressed. Circuses, tradespeople, artists and gypsies either commissioned new caravans or purchased used ones in the mid-1800s as public caravan services ceased. Toll roads began to be abolished in the late 1800s, reducing the cost of road travel and giving a further boost to private caravan traffic. This led to something of a caravan free-for-all on the roads, lanes and commons of Britain. To make matters worse, those left behind by the Industrial Revolution, particularly the poor and unemployed, joined the entertainers and the gypsies in using caravans as permanent, low-cost housing. Caravans belonged to people with no fixed abode, living on the periphery of Victorian society with few rights and no status. Static caravan communities grew up on the edge of towns and cities with poor sanitation and sick inhabitants. Horse-drawn caravans and their occupants were seen as a curse.

The Caravan Curse

The portrayal of caravans in nineteenth-century literature reflected Victorian society's ambivalence towards these motley vehicles and their users. In Charles Dickens' 1840 novel *The Old Curiosity Shop*, the caravan of waxworks proprietress Mrs Jarley was one of the earliest to appear in Victorian literature. It was extensively described by Dickens:

'It was not a shabby, dingy, dusty cart, but a smart little house upon wheels, with white dimity curtains festooning the windows, and window-shutters of green picked out with panels of a staring red, in which happily-contrasted colours the whole concern shone brilliant.'

Dickens notes that the interior of Mrs Jarley's caravan was 'constructed after the fashion of a berth on board ship', an early reference to the influence of ship accommodation on caravan design. But Mrs Jarley herself was portrayed as a lady who, although 'kind and considerate' suffered from 'a lowness of spirits' that required a constant stimulant from 'a suspicious bottle'.

Suspicion of caravan occupants in late Victorian Britain was reflected in newspapers of the time. Reporters writing around

Mrs. Jarley's caravan, from Charles Dickens' *The Old Curiosity Shop* (UK, 1840)

1880 filled their columns with caravan horror stories including caravan murders, fires, asphyxiation and outbreaks of smallpox. One newspaper called caravans 'travelling fever houses'. Over time, suspicion led to harassment. Gypsy encampments were subject to constant persecution, being raided on a regular basis by police seeking the perpetrators of alleged chicken-stealing and other petty crimes. Local communities would seek to have nearby encampments removed. Sanitation inspectors visited caravan settlements, both gypsy and non-gypsy, to impose fines or bans on 'unsanitary' caravans. Scottish local councils complained about caravans being on the roads on Sundays, blaming the English for a lack of respect for the day of rest.

By 1885 public unease amongst the more conservative elements of British society over the status of caravans reached

Above: An engraving entitled 'Homeless' from the *Illustrated London News* of 3 January 1874, depicting a family made homeless by a caravan fire (UK, 1874)

Right: Miss Evelyn Hope and girl in *The Sketch* of 7 August 1907, depicting the romance of caravanning. Over 30 or so years, the image of caravanning was transformed from a curse to an idyllic way of life (UK, 1907)

a peak. Several moves to legislate against the construction and movement of 'mobile dwellings' were attempted. Whilst these were ultimately unsuccessful, it was clear that caravan owners had come to be viewed as antisocial fringe-dwellers. This was not an atmosphere conducive to taking a caravan for a relaxing holiday, and yet it is about this time that the first holiday caravanners took to British country roads. Over the next thirty years, these pioneers would make caravanning if not respectable, then at least tolerable.

The First Recreational Caravans

The first-known mention in print of a British, purpose-built, recreational caravan occurred in the *Illustrated Land and Water* newspaper of 20 March 1872 under the heading of 'A Novel Expedition':

'It is intended, we are assured, by a party of gentlemen not unknown to the sporting and literary world, to shortly embark on an expedition round England and Scotland, visiting and sojourning in some of the most untrodden districts of the island. This grand tour is to be made in caravans, built expressly for the purpose. They are to be fitted up with stoves, mirrors, couches, cooking utensils, and every other requisite, to which may be added guns, angling rods, and a flight of trained falcons.'

No records have yet come to light of these caravans ever being built. It was not uncommon for newspapers of the time to report plans which never came to pass. Still, this report offers evidence that the concept of a purpose-built, recreational caravan was in the minds of a group of hunting gentlemen as early as 1872.

The benefits of a caravan holiday were raised a few years later in 1880. When reflecting on the prosperous lot of a travelling coconut shy owner (a fairground attraction where balls are thrown at coconuts on poles), a newspaper reporter mused:

'The happy occupant of a caravan has no rent or taxes to pay; he has perpetual change of scene; he may generally, if he likes, make enough money to keep him comfortable. Indeed, it would be rather a pleasant thing for persons who do not want to make money to live in a caravan for the fun and pleasure of the thing. It wouldn't be a bad experiment for an autumn holiday, and those who once got accustomed to such a Nomad life might decide to stick to it.'

The *East Anglian Daily Times,* 27 August 1880

In 1883 the first confirmation of a caravan holiday appeared in the press. The trip was made by two sons of the Earl of Essex:

'The sons of the Earl of Essex, who have for some time been travelling through North Wales in a large caravan, arriving in Ruabon gipsy fashion, have wended their way through the valley and over the mountains, via the Vale of Llangollen and the Snowdonian district. Halting on the Castle square at Carnarvon, however, the visitors were ordered to 'move on' by a zealous policeman, because of large crowds collecting. Their tour in the Principality has created much excitement and amusement.'

The *Sheffield and Rotherham Independent,*
3 August 1883

Other newspaper accounts of the same journey add more colour, including the fact that the caravan was painted yellow and that the Earl's sons had roast hedgehog and trout for dinner, served on a silver plate. It was further reported that the caravan was a 'show caravan', suggesting that the caravan was borrowed or hired from a travelling show rather than being purpose-built. In 1885 there were reports of other caravan holidays in Scotland and Cornwall. Common to all such reports is the nature of the participants – they were all wealthy gentlemen who had discovered a new way to spend some of their leisure time. By the late 1880s, the hitherto hostile mood in some parts of the press was starting to change, with caravans considered in a more favourable light:

'The caravan life, whether sanitary or insanitary, has something very fascinating about it.'

The *Graphic,* 14 April 1888

The reason for this change in attitude was due almost entirely to the efforts of one man, whose 'gypsy' travels were widely documented and reported upon. The man was Dr William Gordon Stables. His caravan of 1885 called *The Wanderer* was, as far as we currently know, the first, purpose-built recreational vehicle in the world.

The Wanderer

A Scottish naval surgeon forced into early retirement through illness, Dr William Gordon Stables became a prolific writer of boys' adventure stories and books on the subjects of health and pets. He commissioned *The Wanderer* in about 1884 from the Bristol Wagon Works Company at a cost of £300 in order to explore the country, improve his health and write. Calling it a 'land yacht', Stables modelled the caravan interior on a yacht cabin, using a design that was simple, efficient and well organized. The layout was doubtless based on his personal experiences of ship accommodation.

Stables decried the design of what he called 'the old-fashioned caravan' believing it to be cramped, stuffy and poorly sprung. By contrast *The Wanderer* was almost 20ft long, 11ft high and 6ft wide. Though austere by comparison with some of the finest gypsy *vardos* of the day, it was well built. It had an exterior of solid mahogany lined inside with maple, weighed 2 tons when loaded and needed two horses to pull it. As Stables later admitted to Caravan Club Secretary J. Harris Stone, his only regret about the design of *The Wanderer* was that it was 'most uncomfortable', being so heavy and of a construction heritage that had more in common with a Pullman railway carriage than a horse-drawn coach.

Stables gave a detailed account of how *The Wanderer* was used. Of particular interest is the allocation of camping duties among members of Stables' travel party, which in turn influenced the caravan's facilities. *The Wanderer* had a front lounge room, a single sofa bed and an 'after cabin' kitchen at the rear containing a portable Rippingille cooking-range. There was a separate 'after-tent' used 'onshore' for bathing. A coachman called 'John G.' either slept in coaching inns where the horses were stabled or up front in the *coupé*. A young valet called Alfred Foley slept in the 'after cabin'. As well as having the important attribute of not snoring, Foley had to act as 'cook, steward, valet and general factotum'. One of his duties was as a scout, riding ahead of the caravan on a Ranelagh Club tricycle 'tender' to warn those ahead of their movements and to seek out overnight stopping places. Completing the team were two horses called Polly Pea-Blossom and Captain Cornflower, a Newfoundland dog called Hurricane Bob and a West Australian cockatoo called Polly. Stables' party was thus a microcosm of the English class system. The employment of servants on caravan journeys, with separate and generally inferior accommodation, began a trend that other gentlemen gypsies would later follow.

The Wanderer's first major journey took place in 1885 from Stables' home in Twyford, Berkshire to Inverness in Scotland. It was a remarkable distance to cover at the time. The trip was

A photograph entitled *Waiting till the Kettle Boils,* the frontispiece from *The Cruise of the Land Yacht "Wanderer"; or, Thirteen Hundred Miles in my Caravan* by Gordon Stables. The image shows *The Wanderer* with Dr Gordon Stables seated (centre) with his children and dog. Also in the picture are the coachman (left), valet (right) and tricycle (rear) used for scouting out overnight stays and warning other road users of *The Wanderer's* impending arrival (UK, c1885)

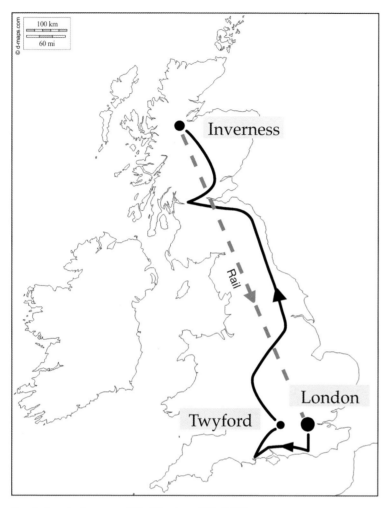

The first major journey of *The Wanderer* (UK, 1885)

train back to London. Still, the curiosity and kindness of strangers on Stables' journey, the beauty of nature and the trip's health-giving properties resulted in what Stables called 'the pleasantest voyage ever I have made in my life'. The round trip was completed in five months by road via the south coast of England and Hampshire's New Forest. Stables continued to explore the English countryside in *The Wanderer* in subsequent years.

It is hard to overstate the contribution of Stables to the development of the recreational vehicle. At a time when living in a caravan was both unfashionable and even dangerous, Stables commissioned the construction of a yacht-inspired caravan and travelled long distances around Britain purely for pleasure. As a former naval surgeon, he was one of the first to espouse the health benefits of living in a caravan (see page 22), and in 1891, the first to conceive the idea of forming a caravan club. Later, as the first vice-president of the UK Caravan Club which formed in 1907, Stables acted as an ambassador for the growing caravan movement until his death in 1910. The publication of the stories of his caravan travels in newspapers around the world introduced this new hobby to a wide audience and inspired countless others to build and travel in horse-drawn caravans for pleasure. Today Dr William Gordon Stables should rightly be known as the Father of the Recreational Vehicle. His most important legacy, *The Wanderer* caravan, has now been fully restored and is owned by the UK Caravan and Motorhome Club.

described in Stables' book, *The Cruise of the Land Yacht "Wanderer"; or, Thirteen Hundred Miles in my Caravan*, published in 1886. In the book Stables gives us a colourful list of the other types of caravan occupants of the day, with whom he was often confused when travelling in *The Wanderer*. The list includes a Salvation Army general, a travelling artist, a photographer, a menagerie, an eccentric baronet, a madman and 'King of The Gypsies'.

One book reviewer of the period expressed dissatisfaction with Stables' account because, in his view, nothing very much happened. But, as Stables himself might have retorted, that was precisely the point of a recreational caravan holiday. Even so, it was in parts an arduous journey that involved climbing the steep Grampian Mountains, becoming bogged in a Scottish field (*The Wanderer* was rescued by local miners) and incurring severe damage to the caravan's contents when it was placed on a goods

The Wanderer is rescued from a field by local miners in Scotland after overnight rain (UK, 1886)

The Gentlemen Gypsies

The Bohemian caravan of The Duke of Newcastle (UK, c1892)

A large and lavish gypsy caravan and its owners (and dog) (UK, 1905)

A caravan called *Maisonette* at a Caravan Club meet in the New Forest. (UK, 1914)

Miss Grace Simmons and party at a Caravan Club meet in the New Forest (UK, 1914)

Between about 1890 and 1914 a trickle of mostly wealthy people took to the country lanes of Britain for leisure trips in commissioned, self-built or hired horse-drawn caravans. As the travels of Stables became more widely known, the trickle turned into a steady flow. These people came to be known as gentlemen gypsies. The caravans were of various designs, some inspired by *The Wanderer* and based on Pullman-style railway coaches or trams, others on ornate gypsy *vardos*.

As recreational caravanning grew in popularity, caravan designs changed. There was a trend away from heavy caravan design typified by *The Wanderer* toward simpler, box-shaped caravans. Although less ornate, these lighter caravans were more practical than their predecessors. They provided more internal space, could be pulled by a single horse and allowed greater access to hilly beauty spots or areas with poor roads.

Although termed gentlemen gypsies, this pioneering group of recreational travellers included many women in their ranks. Guard dogs were common companions and compulsory for ladies travelling alone. Servants and horse attendants came along on many of these journeys but generally slept separately in tents or at coaching inns. Some caravan owners invited genuine Romany gypsies on their travels to learn more of their customs and language. Nearly all caravans had names. After 1907 many became members of the newly-formed Caravan Club, which kept a record of 'pitches' throughout the country where caravans would be welcomed by landowners.

As well as separation of travellers by class on the first horse-drawn caravan holidays, there was also segregation of the sexes. One caravan owner explained to *The Field* newspaper in 1901:

'The ladies (where the party consists of both sexes) sleep inside, and the men in an old Army bell tent… We find the best party to take comprised three ladies (as that does not crowd up the caravan at night) and four men…One man looks after, grooms and feeds the horses, another cooks, and the remaining two divide the water-carrying and wood-cutting…Two of the ladies do the entire washing up, and the third takes the interior of the van under her special care, sweeps it out constantly, and packs everything away as it is handed up to her.'

M. Arnold, *The Field*, 9 November 1901

Some 120 years later, some would argue that the distribution of daily RV tasks between the sexes has changed little.

Lady Grosvenor

One English lady named Helen Sheffield, who later became Lady Arthur Grosvenor, was willing to undertake all the tasks involved in a caravan holiday herself. She became a figure of international attention for her devotion to caravanning and gypsy culture. *The New York Times* of 10 June 1907 explains:

'Lady Arthur Grosvenor, wife of Lord Arthur Grosvenor, brother of the Duke of Westminster, is traveling about the country disguised as a gypsy and calling herself Syeira Lee…Lady Arthur Grosvenor has been playing gypsy since May 27. She is now traveling through Oxfordshire, bound for Ascot. She gets up at 5 o'clock every morning, cooks her own breakfast, and usually takes the road at 8 o'clock. She may possibly write a book on her experiences of gypsy life… An undeniable sensation would be caused by Lady Arthur

Lady Arthur Grosvenor (left) in gypsy clothing with her caravan and two companions (UK, 1908)

Grosvenor's appearance on Ascot Heath with her baskets, kettles and frying pans.'

Lady Grosvenor's transformation into a gypsy, far from being a whim, was part of her firm commitment to gypsy folklore and traditions. She was a strong supporter of the Gypsy Lore Society and later in the 1930s supported gypsies under threat of eviction from Epsom Downs. Her commitment to the gypsy cause created interest in the United States and Australia and would have caused many to wonder what was so special about this lifestyle for a titled lady to forego her privileges, wake up at five a.m. and cook her own breakfast.

The Furniture Caravan Maker

At the turn of the twentieth century the first, dedicated, horse-drawn caravan makers appeared. One of the earliest was Bertram Smith. He started building caravans in 1898, initially for his own use. Like Lady Grosvenor, he was a more egalitarian caravanner than the gentlemen gypsies but reportedly quite eccentric. His travel habits were said to include posing as a tourist and sending postcards to imaginary people. On one occasion it is said he was arrested for being a dangerous lunatic. His caravan designs were entirely rational however, with his first being 18ft long and weighing only 1 ton, half the weight of *The Wanderer*. By 1907 he was running a fleet of hire caravans disparagingly called 'furniture vans' by some gentlemen gypsies because of their simplicity. They were built using thin wooden panels and canvas on a lightweight chassis and axles. Each had three rooms – a bedroom, dining room and kitchen, the latter with removable wall panels to provide extra ventilation and for alternative use as a veranda.

Smith wrote one of the earliest books on caravanning in 1907 called *The Whole Art of Caravanning*. Like Dr Gordon Stables he was a strong advocate of the outdoor life, but unlike Stables he did most of the cooking himself. He travelled the countryside in his own horse-drawn caravan called *Triumvir*. By shunning the heavy ornamentation of gypsy *vardos* in favour of simplicity and practicality, Smith was a pioneer of the lightweight caravans that would become so important in the popularisation of caravanning in the motoring age.

Bertram Smith's *Triumvir* (UK, 1907)

The simple interior of Bertram Smith's *Triumvir* (UK, 1907)

Bertram Hutchings

Bertram Hutchings was another pioneer in the development of lightweight caravans. Hutchings had a knack for intelligent caravan design that carried him successfully into the motoring era. Hutchings owned a health food shop in Winchester in Hampshire. Enamoured with the outdoor life after a summer camping holiday in 1911, Hutchings and his new wife bravely spent the following winter in an 18-foot, horse-drawn caravan that Hutchings later described as built 'in the days when brute force and ignorance were the principal stock-in-trade of the caravan builders'. Convinced he could build something better with the help of relatives in the coach-building business, in 1912 Hutchings decided to produce a short, horse-drawn caravan of his own.

Receiving favourable reactions to the van, Hutchings went on to build a small fleet of similar caravans that were made available for hire at £5 per week and £1 for a horse. Unlike gypsy *vardos*, the walls of his caravans were straight and the entry door was at the side. Hutchings built his short, light caravans until the outbreak of the First World War.

An important stimulus to the growth of the caravan hobby was the sharing of information between caravan owners on places to stay overnight. In the absence of caravan parks, owners were reliant on the goodwill of private landowners. The availability of a list of caravan 'pitches' was a key reason for members to join the first caravan clubs.

The first horse-drawn caravan built by Bertram Hutchings in the New Forest (UK, 1912)

J. Harris Stone and The Caravan Club

'There is one wholesome lesson everyone learns when caravanning – to think more, to talk less.'

from *Caravanning and Camping Out* by
J. Harris Stone (1914)

J. Harris Stone was probably the first caravan philosopher. He was the Honorary Secretary of The Caravan Club of Great Britain and Ireland from its formation in 1907 to 1935 and its Vice President from 1935 to 1939. Although trained as a barrister he was a keen caravanner, promoting the virtues of a caravan life in his 1914 book *Caravanning and Camping Out*. The book is not only a practical guide to the outdoor life, but also a philosophical one, including many perceptive comments which are still relevant today.

As a founding member of The Caravan Club, Harris Stone would organize annual caravan meetings, document all the caravans present along with their owners and create lists of sites for the use of club members where caravans might pitch their vans with the consent of private landowners.

The arrival of the first motorhomes in Britain in the early 1900s presented a dilemma for the club. Although the club officially welcomed all types of RVs, Harris Stone was a horse-drawn caravan advocate. He felt that motorhomes defeated the whole purpose of caravanning. His caravanning philosophy was to travel slowly, go off the beaten track, observe nature in all its glory and meet others of a similar persuasion. He felt motorhomes were too fast and heavy to achieve these aims. He was particularly scathing of the early motorhome manufacturers:

'The builders of motor caravans seem to me to be unable to get away from the trammels of their business, to depart from the traditions of mahogany-panelled vehicles, with enormously strong and stout ribs, bracings and absurdly heavy fittings, which have come down to them from the days of the old family coach, through a sojourn in the dust-loving and cumbrous compartments of a main-line, first class railway carriage.'

After the First World War ended, The Caravan Club suffered a loss of membership and interest. Horses were hard to come by and caravan production had paused. The industry was in any event moving away from the heavy, labour-intensive, horse-drawn caravan towards the new leisure opportunities offered by motorized transport. In 1935 the club was relaunched for a new generation of caravan owners, with Harris Stone as its Vice President. Today the club is called The Caravan and Motorhome Club and is Europe's largest touring organization.

J. Harris Stone, the first secretary of the Caravan Club (UK, 1907)

The Camping and Caravanning Club

Thomas Hiram Holding was a keen camper, cyclist and canoeist and is widely regarded as the father of modern leisure camping. In 1878 he formed the Cyclists' Touring Club and developed lightweight camping equipment that could be carried on a cycle. His 1898 book *Cycle and Camp in Connemara* explained why camping holidays were healthier and cheaper than staying in hotels and described in detail the equipment needed for a cycle camping holiday. Following a positive response to the book, Holding formed The Association of Cycle Campers ('ACC') in 1901 starting with twelve members, growing to over 100 members in 1902 and over 800 by 1910. The association held annual camps (divided into bachelors', married couples' and ladies' quarters), camp displays and tent-pitching competitions. Holding wrote the influential *Campers' Handbook* in 1908.

The ACC was on friendly terms with its sister organisation, The Caravan Club, as demonstrated when ACC members were invited to bring their tents to The Caravan Club's first annual meet in 1908. There was some overlap between the two organisations, with members of the ACC, including Holding, designing their own tent trailers and caravans incorporating their knowledge of lightweight cycle camping materials and techniques. Both organisations fought successfully against the anti-camping Moveable Dwelling Bill of 1908-10 and worked to create formalized camping areas throughout the country. Caravan owners were welcome to join the ACC from its inception and were granted their own Caravan Section in 1933. Following a number of name changes, the name 'The Camping and Caravanning Club' was adopted in 1983. Today the organisation has over 700,000 members.

Thomas Hiram Holding (UK, 1908)

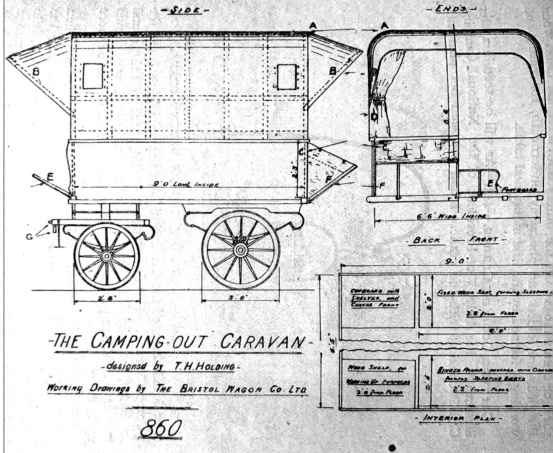

A 'camping out caravan' design by Holding published in *The Campers' Handbook* (UK, 1908)

The First Motorhomes (1905-1920)

The arrival of the automobile at the turn of the century brought with it new opportunities but also difficult decisions for Britain's early RV adopters. Should they continue to use horses or switch to horsepower? Unlike France, Britain had overlooked steam power as a source of RV power, primarily because traction engines were associated in the UK with agricultural and road building work. The gentlemen gypsies were seeking to escape the Industrial Revolution, not take it with them. Furthermore, powered vehicles were too heavy to reach the remote camping areas favoured by horse-drawn caravan owners. On the other hand, horses needed feeding, stabling and general care, duties usually carried out by a valet or horse handler who needed both wages and accommodation.

It was the First World War that resolved the issue decisively in favour of the internal combustion engine. By 1914 the affordability and power of automobiles were important factors in their growing popularity. It was however the high number of horse deaths during the war, estimated at some eight million, that sealed the fate of the horse-drawn caravan. Despite a horse shortage there was a temporary resurgence in the use of horse-drawn vehicles after the First World War as the motorized transport industry got back on its feet. But throughout the 1920s horse-drawn caravan numbers declined, surviving only as a niche tourism market that still exists today.

The first motorhome to be seen on British roads was probably the *Passe Partout* of France in 1902 (see page 76). A few spectators in London would have had their first ever glimpse of a motorhome as the *Passe Partout* started out on its ambitious journey around the world.

The first 'motor caravan' or motorhome to be constructed in Britain was probably that of J.W. Mallalieu. It was built by the Belsize Motor Co. of Manchester in about 1905. Mallalieu was a wealthy bedding manufacturer from Liverpool who commissioned a motorhome that comprised three compartments – a dining area, sleeping area and a kitchen. It also had a WC with running water. A total of six beds were available. The motorhome weighed 4 tons fully laden, had solid tyres back and front and was driven by a 40hp petrol engine. With an average speed of 9mph, the motorhome would have been rather slow and uncomfortable. Nevertheless, Mallalieu took the motorhome on family holidays as far away as Wales and Scotland.

Politician and Austin director Harvey du Cros commissioned a motorhome from the Austin Motor Company a few years later. It was exhibited at the London Motor Show in 1909 and cost a not inconsiderable £2,000. The motorhome's panels were made of aluminium, helping to keep the weight down to a 'mere' 2.5 tons. In true gentleman gypsy style, du Cros took with him a servant and a cook, whose sleeping quarters were box beds on the roof, accessible by ladder and covered with canvas. There was also rooftop seating for a few brave passengers. The motorhome's interior was rather more sumptuous and included a telephone for speaking with the chauffeur, electric lighting, ventilator fans and rattle-proof cabinets for china, glass, cutlery and silver.

Early motorhome owners would often take separate tents with them to supplement their living space or to segregate the sexes. Some began experimenting with canvas attached to the vehicle. One example was the motorhome belonging to W.M. Appleton, nicknamed *The Aeroplane*. It made regular appearances at Caravan Club meetings. It was given its nickname because, according to Club Secretary J. Harris Stone:

'outside blinds are provided all round the car, which roll up snug when not in use... these are held in place with bamboo rods and light stay-cords...When pitched, and all the blinds are spread out around it, the vehicle bears a striking likeness to some of those aerial carriages now becoming so familiar to us all.'

The Belsize Motor Company motorhome of J.W. Mallalieu (UK, c1905)

The Austin Motor Company's 40hp motor caravan of Harvey du Cros (UK, 1909)

Appleton was therefore one of the first RV owners to use the now ubiquitous awning.

Enthusiastic early motorhome owners would sometimes purchase more than one vehicle. They would work with manufacturers, suggesting improved layouts and facilities based on personal experience. Albert Fletcher, a wealthy mill owner and Caravan Club member from Ashton-under-Lyne, owned both horse-drawn caravans and motorhomes. His first motorhome was built in 1906 on a 40hp Ryknield chassis and was noted for its rooftop seating area. Fletcher's second motorhome, built in 1913 on a 40hp Daimler chassis, was a design derived from personal experience during 18,000 miles of travel in his first motorhome. The second vehicle repeated the rooftop feature of the original and kept its two rooms but switched the sleeping room to the rear and brought the entrance to the centre. With more elaborate bodywork by renowned gypsy and living van builder Orton & Sons, the Daimler travelled at 12mph, weighed 5 tons and consumed fuel at the rate of 5 miles per gallon.

W.M. Appleton's *Aeroplane* (UK, c1910)

Below: Albert Fletcher (third from left) and J. Harris Stone (second from left) pictured with Fletcher's 1913 40hp Daimler chassis motor caravan at The Caravan Club's 1914 New Forest Meet at Cadnam (UK, 1914)

Inset: The first motorhome of Albert Fletcher built on a 40hp Ryknield chassis (UK, 1906)

Not perhaps impressive by today's standards, but still faster and cheaper to run than horses.

After the First World War motorhomes continued to be produced in small numbers for generally wealthy clients but were hampered in design terms by their truck ancestry. When motorhomes first appeared in the UK from about 1905, they were seen by many as the natural successor to the horse-drawn caravan. But early motorhomes were heavy, noisy, slow, expensive, unreliable and built only to order using a harsh truck chassis as their foundation. Matters improved slightly after the First World War as reliability, weight and prices improved, but according to caravan historian W. M. Whiteman:

'The motor caravans of the first post-war years were much lighter than those built before 1914, but they were not very reliable, they were very cramped, they had little road advantage over the trailer because of the universal speed limit, and the horsepower tax made them unattractive. Faced with growing competition from trailer caravans, the motor caravan almost fizzled out.'

from *The History of The Caravan* by
W.M. Whiteman (1973)

The so-called 'horsepower tax', which came into effect in 1921, penalized motor vehicles with larger engines. This reduced the attractiveness of motorhomes (with more powerful engines) compared to caravans towed by lower-powered automobiles. So, after an initial post-war flourish in the 1920s, motorhomes fell out of general favour – they were found to be emperors with no clothes. Despite the occasional design flourish, they would not revive in any numbers until lightweight truck and van chassis became available at reasonable cost some thirty years later in the 1950s.

Early British Caravans (1914-1924)

As the first motorhomes were lumbering slowly along in the early 1900s, what would prove to be their major competitor in RV terms was coming to life. The idea of towing a caravan behind a motor vehicle almost certainly originated in France with Émile Levassor's 1895 concept for a caravan towed by a petrol automobile, closely followed by the French steam-drawn coaches of the late 1890s (see pages 72-75). During the early 1900s Britain's RV pioneers remained largely enamoured with the romance and tranquillity of horse-drawn caravans. But although this strong tradition may have given pause for thought before replacing the horse with an automobile, it was for the British no major hurdle. The design of the first motor-drawn caravans in Britain after the First World War was influenced by two different forms of wartime transport. These distinguished British motor-drawn caravans from those of other countries and gave Britain an early lead in the development of this novel form of RV.

The first design influence was the trailer ambulance. Developed in Edgbaston, Birmingham by E.M. Tailby in 1914 to carry two stretchers, the trailer ambulance was used to transfer the wounded between British railway stations and local hospitals. It had similar advantages to the nineteenth century ambulance wagon of the USA, being both lightweight and comfortable, and, according to an assessment in the British Medical Journal, 'does not curtail the seating accommodation in the vehicle'. According to British RV historian Andrew Jenkinson, the ease of towing ambulance trailers was noticed by Bill Riley junior of Birmingham-based manufacturer Eccles, Britain's first large-scale maker of caravans towed by automobiles.

The second design influence was the aircraft trailer. These were canvas-covered trailers used during the war to transport disassembled aircraft between factories and airfields. They were

---

Speed Limits

Following the abolition in 1896 of the requirement for motor vehicles to be preceded by a man walking with a red flag, the UK road speed limit was raised that year to 4mph on the open road with local authorities setting their own limits, typically 10-15mph. The national speed limit was raised to 20mph in 1903 and then abolished altogether in 1930, except for most caravans which were limited to 30mph. Within a few years the caravan speed limit became a burden to everyone. Motorists who got stuck behind slow caravans became frustrated whilst those towing caravans could go faster mechanically but were not allowed. The low speed of 30mph also meant that towing stability at higher speeds was not adequately considered in trailer design until the 1950s.

The ambulance trailer developed by E.M. Tailby (UK, c1914)

The first Eccles caravan (UK, 1919)

Aircraft trailers on display in Paris on Bastille Day (France, 1913)

A Piggott Bros. caravan with Armstrong Siddeley automobile (UK, 1922)

light enough to be towed by some of the low-powered automobiles and trucks of the day and served as a design inspiration for the first canvas caravans of Piggott Bros., another early British caravan manufacturer.

After the First World War, war-weary Britain needed a holiday. Motor-drawn caravans were a new means of escaping to the country for a few days at low cost using the family automobile, but entrepreneurs were needed to build them. The Navarac Caravan Company ('caravan' spelled backwards) was the first British company to build caravans on a limited scale. It did so by accident. Formed in 1919 by Richard St Barbe Baker, Navarac saw an opportunity to make leisure vehicles out of

Alcock's Streamlined Caravan

Frederick Alcock's streamlined caravan (UK, 1914)

One of the earliest British motor-drawn caravans seems to have been influenced by nothing other than its owner's imagination. Standing in remarkable design isolation to the other caravans of the day is Frederick Alcock's self-built caravan, said to have been built in 1914. It could be mistaken for a caravan from the 1930s. Towed by a 38hp Lanchester and itself mounted on a Lanchester axle from 1909, the caravan had a streamlined roof and all-round square windows. Closer inspection of the caravan suggests it was finished rather crudely, and its weight and interior layout are unknown. Photographs of Alcock's caravan were only published in 1969, making authentication of its construction date challenging.

A four-wheeled Navarac caravan made from aircraft parts (UK, 1919)

surplus First World War aircraft equipment. Submitting what he though was a derisory offer to the Government Disposals Board for enough material to build one or two caravans, St Barbe Baker was amazed to find that not only was his offer accepted, but that he was given enough surplus equipment to fill ten railway trucks. The Navarac caravan was built on two aircraft axles, had a timber chassis and contained a cooking range, rooftop water tank, ice chest, grocery lockers, awnings, tents and camp beds. It could also be horse-drawn, weighing about 1.8 tons. However, St Barbe Baker's passions lay elsewhere in forestry and conservation and the company lasted less than a year.

Caravans towed by automobiles took some time to gain traction with consumers. Greedy hotel owners were taking advantage of the post-war holiday boom at seaside resorts and country towns by increasing their prices. So-called 'trailer caravans' were the perfect alternative – towable by small automobiles, detachable at camp for local tours in the tow vehicle and rentable by the week at reasonable cost. They were even touted by some as the solution to the post-war housing crisis, although semi-permanent caravans did not fully evolve as a concept until after the Second World War. The main problem with trailer caravans was their novelty.

Nevertheless, at the beginning of the 1920s, three trailer caravan manufacturers went into limited production – Eccles, Piggott Bros. and Bertram Hutchings, all starting within a few months of each other. Two of the three, Eccles and Hutchings, would go on to become household names in the British caravan industry. With no precedents to follow, these pioneers were forced to experiment with caravan design, materials and technologies. The 1920s thus became the decade of experimentation. Meanwhile, the heavy and unreliable motorhome refused to die, kept on life support by a few creative builders.

The name of Eccles is synonymous with the early British caravan industry. Eccles was the first company in the world to manufacture caravans on a large scale and the first to recognize the need to promote the caravan lifestyle as much as its vans. Formed as Eccles Motor Transport Ltd in 1919 by W.A.J. Riley and his son W.J. Riley, the company assumed control of a traditional transport business belonging to H.A. Eccles. Whilst Riley senior, who had produced a primitive motorhome in 1913, thought motorhomes represented the future, Riley junior was a firm believer in caravan trailers. After displaying both a motorhome and caravan trailer outside the 1919 London Motor Show and receiving an order for the trailer from a countess, father and son decided to prioritize the trailer.

Eccles found sales initially hard to come by, since the first steel-built caravans were not very attractive and most people did not understand their purpose.

Following a more encouraging response to their revised plywood caravan design shown at the British Industries Fair in 1921, Eccles started significant production in 1922. The company began promoting their caravans through street tours, leaflets and free inspections with the assistance of its appointed dealers and hire companies. Advertising in the general as well as motoring newspapers reached a broader audience, whilst journalists enthusiastically advocated the 'gypsy holiday' using what today would be called advertorials. The decision to manufacture caravans for hire was an Eccles masterstroke, since curious potential buyers could find out if they liked the new caravan lifestyle before buying.

In the mid-1920s, the lantern roof (a raised central roof with slot windows) helped to brighten the interior and provide ventilation. Jacobean-style leadlight windows were added to luxury models to make them look more 'homely'. These domestic touches were hallmarks of Eccles caravans, taking early designs away from their ambulance trailer roots and bringing them closer to a 'house on wheels', leaving consumers in no doubt as to their purpose.

An Eccles caravan (unknown location, 1922)

Whilst Eccles is the company most people associate with early English caravans, another shorter-lived company, Piggott Bros., focused on lightweight caravans that combined their prior experience in tent-making with an idea from the aviation industry – the aircraft trailer.

The aircraft trailer was in effect a tent on wheels. Noticing that there were many such trailers available for next to nothing after the war, Piggott Bros. decided to turn them into lightweight caravans using canvas stretched across simple ash and oak frames. Piggott Bros. patented the idea, along with a number of other caravan innovations such as extending rear platforms and folding bay windows.

In 1920 Piggott Bros. were the first company to formally exhibit caravans at the London Motor Show. They exhibited both canvas and plywood-walled models equipped with a range of basic creature comforts including lantern roofs,

windows, curtains, mattresses, oil stoves and electric lighting. In keeping with their camping roots, Piggott Bros. offered customers wanting an indoor toilet nothing more than a seat over a hole in the floor that had to be lined up with a hole in the ground. Piggott Bros. continued making improvements to their caravans until about 1925, after which they decided to return to their main business of tent and marquee manufacturing.

The first motor-drawn caravans commonly used axles from other vehicles, including from aircraft trailers, aircraft and automobiles. It soon became clear however that these were not fit for purpose. They were unable to withstand the weight and the sustained vibrations from a laden caravan on tow and as a result often collapsed. The longer-lived caravan manufacturers started making purpose-built axles. But whether by design or accident, caravans assembled from lightweight parts of other

The Piggott caravan display at a UK motor show (UK, 1924)

vehicles had opened up a significant new market. Because they could be towed by automobiles with low-powered engines, owners of small automobiles could use them. Single-axle caravans were also technically more straightforward and cheaper to make than four-wheeled versions. The cost and weight advantages of trailer caravans over motorhomes set in train a thirty-year period when the trailer caravan would come to dominate the motorhome in the UK.

Early Trailer Caravan Experimentation

Experimentation to find the best design for trailer caravans continued apace in the mid-1920s. One experiment (first seen in France in 1920) was the caravan designed on the 'telescopic principle' where a caravan body was split into top and bottom halves. The top half of the van dropped over the bottom, reducing overall height under tow. It was thought that, as automobiles became more powerful and faster, wind resistance would become a factor. The ability to see behind the caravan whilst under tow was also seen as a safety advantage.

Shadow Caravans were an early example of this design. They were manufactured by R.H. Sievwright and Co. of Wolverhampton from about 1925 onwards. The upper section of

the van was raised on site using chains, whilst overall caravan width was reduced to minimize wind resistance. Although Shadows met with some success following their exhibition at the London Motor Shows of 1928 and 1929, the telescopic mechanism was, according to RV historian W.M. Whiteman, prone to failure and the roof subject to leaks.

Telescopic caravans were also made by Eccles in the late 1920s. Like the Shadow, the Eccles telescopic caravan had solid walls but was wider and therefore more wind resistant than the Shadow. The design became outdated when its main safety advantage of good rear vision under tow was overtaken by the provision of see-through windows in full height caravans.

Complex trailer caravan designs added weight, negating one of the trailer caravan's advantages over the motorhome. Simplicity was the key to light weight. Eccles was fast learning this lesson as low-powered but affordable automobiles such as the 7hp Austin or Jowett became popular. These vehicles could tow only lightweight caravans. In 1927, to illustrate the lightness of their smaller caravans, Eccles designed a caravan that could be towed by a motorcycle.

Bertram Hutchings was another manufacturer keen to experiment with RV design. Unburdened with heavy coachbuilding traditions, Hutchings was one of the few British RV manufacturers to make a successful transition from the

A Shadow collapsible caravan (open) 'harnessed' to a Clyno car ... (UK, 1927)

... and in closed position ready for the road (UK, 1927)

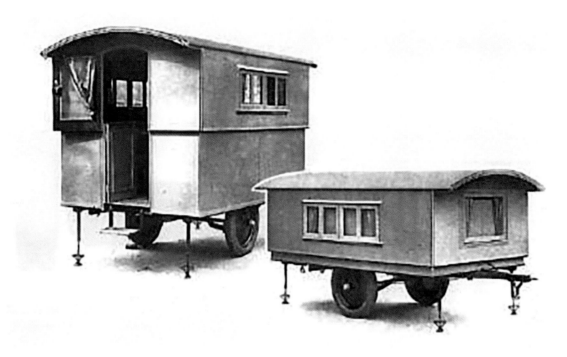

An Eccles collapsible caravan (UK, 1929)

An Eccles motorcycle caravan (UK, 1927)

An early Bertram Hutchings motor-drawn caravan (UK, 1920)

horse-drawn to the motorized era. After the First World War, Hutchings continued to build 21ft wooden caravans for horse-drawn or semi-permanent use under the Concord brand. Hutchings realized however that the RV market was going through a transition phase towards the motorized RV, so from 1921, he started to experiment with caravans towed by automobiles. His first designs were similar to his box-shaped horse vans, and in the same year he experimented with a 'part-collapsible', four-wheeled caravan that never went into full production. In 1924 Hutchings had more success with the Voyageur caravan, which had curved sides and roof and rear

leadlight bay windows. The Voyageur sold well and remained in production until 1930. Towards the end of the decade Hutchings introduced further new designs including a 7.5ft-long caravan called the Tom Thumb. It was designed to be towed by 7hp automobiles such as the Austin and the Jowett and featured an innovative floor that could be lowered. Hutchings added to his caravan range with the modest Nimblette and the deluxe Lady Nimble. Hutchings tried his hand at lightweight tent trailers, but these did not have the success that they enjoyed in a number of other countries such as the USA and Australia, primarily due to the vagaries of the British weather.

A rare Bertram Hutchings four-wheeled caravan. Little is known about this 10ft 6in long caravan, but the top canvas section may have lowered to reduce wind resistance under tow (UK, 1921)

The influence of ship accommodation on recreational caravan design had been apparent since *The Wanderer*. Naval architect Melville Hart's Flatavan company ('flat in a van') used maritime inspiration for some of his RVs between 1923 and 1934. His Caravan Deluxe of 1924 looked externally like a box on wheels, but inside it contained a well-appointed living room, folding furniture and plenty of storage space. As with a ship's cabin, everything had its place and no space was wasted. Its main claim to fame was an even closer link to the sea – it could be converted into a houseboat by relocating the box section onto a floating pontoon.

In 1926 Hart built a caravan for journalist and politician Sir Harry Brittain called *Colomen Wen*. It was made of fabric covered plywood but was apparently still very heavy due to its height, overhead water tanks, flush lavatory, coal stove and double-bed settee. Especially for wealthier newcomers to the hobby, cooking and washing facilities were essential. The extra weight added to caravans by inclusion of such creature comforts became less of an issue during the late 1920s as tow vehicles of the day became increasingly powerful.

A smaller, hybrid camper trailer appeared in 1925. It was the Rice Folding Caravan, designed by J. Cecil Rice of Yorkshire and manufactured for about a decade starting in 1928. Instead of the collapsible roof used by Shadow and Eccles, its roof lifted and side panels swung out sideways, with canvas protecting the area between the sides and the roof. Internal seating could be converted into two or three beds. As a lightweight camper trailer, it was popular with owners of low-powered cars such as the Austin 7. As Bertram Hutchings had discovered, camper trailers would meet with a mixed reception in the UK, but the Folding Caravan was exported successfully to a number of countries with less variable climates than the UK including Australia and South Africa. Even so, it was no cheaper to manufacture than a standard caravan, making profits difficult to generate when consumers believed that, as a glamorous form of tent, it should be priced accordingly.

A caravan called *Colomen Wen* ('white dove' in Welsh) built by Flatavan for Sir Harry Brittain (UK, 1926)

Above: The Rice Folding Caravan extended (UK, 1936)

Left: The Rice Folding Caravan (UK, 1925)

Motorhomes (1920-1933)

During the 1920s most trailer caravan designs were being increasingly targeted at working families with small automobiles. The motorhome on the other hand was becoming a niche product for the wealthy. Eccles and Hutchings had soon realised the mass market appeal of the trailer caravan but hedged their bets in an emergent and unpredictable new market by making motorhomes in small numbers. Hutchings manufactured a number of motorhomes during the decade, mostly sparsely designed and furnished to keep weight down. Elegant in their simplicity, Hutchings' motorhome interiors could be mistaken for the inside of a country cottage.

As well as producing caravans, Eccles was the most significant of the British motorhome manufacturers of the 1920s, producing a range of vehicles to suit different tastes and budgets. A 1923 Eccles motorhome on a 4.5-litre, 24hp Sunbeam chassis was simple, elegant and designed to appeal to customers of ordinary means. Eccles would sometimes place a new motorhome body on an older chassis to keep costs down.

At the other end of the luxury scale was a gargantuan motorhome built for the Indian Maharajah of Gwalior. Melville Hart of Flatavan built at least three RVs for the Maharajah between 1923 and 1929. The 1926 vehicle was an unusual motorhome and caravan combination containing dining and sleeping accommodation for sixteen people. It was taken to Buckingham Palace for inspection by the King and Queen before delivery. Sales to prestigious clients were often listed in company brochures or at exhibitions and gave invaluable publicity to the manufacturer.

Most UK motorhomes of this period were known as 'conversions', which is to say that a box-shaped body would be placed on a truck or bus chassis behind the engine and driving compartment. A coach-built motorhome, on the other hand, was a single, purpose-built RV body containing both engine and accommodation. As far as we currently know, the first coach-built motorhomes were developed by Charles Louvet of France from about 1923 (see pages 88-94). Probably the first such British motorhome appeared in 1927 and was called the Road Yacht.

'[Pemberton Billing] has taken a six cylinder Erskine chassis, lengthened a few feet for the purpose, and upon it he has mounted a bodywork that looks like a Brobdingnagian garden slug.'

The *Tatler*, 14 September 1927

Above: The interior of a Bertram Hutchings motorhome (UK, early 1920s)

Right: An early Bertram Hutchings motorhome (UK, early 1920s)

A 1922/23 Sunbeam Eccles motorhome (UK, c1923)

A retouched photo of a deluxe Flatavan motorhome and caravan combination built for the Indian Maharajah of Gwalior leaving Buckingham Palace in London after inspection by the King and Queen (UK, 1926)

The interior of the deluxe Flatavan (UK, 1926)

Noel Pemberton Billing's Road Yacht (UK,1927)

Whether or not one agrees with the *Tatler's* assessment of this motorhome, Noel Pemberton Billing's Road Yacht of 1927 made a dramatic departure from the truck-based motorhomes that preceded it. It was an early coach-built motorhome and as far as we know only one was built. It was so radical in its design that nobody bought it. It was a decade ahead of its time.

Its builder, Noel Pemberton Billing, was a maverick British aviator, inventor, writer and politician. His main claim to fame was his role in a sensational libel trial in 1918 in which he asserted that 47,000 high-ranking British 'perverts' were being blackmailed by Germany. No less colourfully, his engineering feats included the development of flying boats, unbreakable gramophone records and a spy camera. According to his biographer Barbara Stoney, none was hugely successful.

Pemberton Billing's Road Yacht was built on a US Erskine Six chassis with a 17hp engine. It had a tea table and wine storage in front of the driver's seat, a bookcase, writing desk, gramophone and radio, electric stove and a fridge. There were twin beds separated into male and female cabins, a bath, a shower and a lavatory. There was hot running water, electric lights and carpet throughout. Despite advertising the motorhome for sale in the UK for 375 guineas, it did not sell. A planned promotional tour of the vehicle to the USA was cancelled at the last minute when Pemberton Billing managed to get financing for a stage play he had written. Its appearance, low-powered engine and top speed of 45mph may have been contributing factors to its lack of appeal, but its main drawback was that its inventor had too many other irons in the fire to spend the necessary time promoting such a radical vehicle to a sceptical public.

Barbara Stoney relates that during a three-year stay in the USA in the early 1930s Pemberton Billing did finally ship the motorhome there to seek a market for it, but by that time the Great Depression had taken hold and it was too expensive for most. Pemberton Billing was forced to sell his motorhome in the USA for 'a ridiculously low sum' in 1933 to help finance his trip home.

A British motorhome that was not short of horsepower appeared in 1933. One of the most powerful vehicles built up to that time, the six-wheeled motorhome built for His Highness Abbas Hilmi II, the ex-Khedive of Egypt (the Khedive was an Ottoman viceroy), was impressive. It had power to the four rear wheels, low pressure tyres, a Leyland Terrier 100hp engine and coachwork made by the Eastern Counties Omnibus Co. It is a forerunner of the almost indestructible off-road RV that was later typified by Australia's OKA Motor Company and demonstrated Britain's early prowess in this field. The interior, tastefully finished in mahogany with silk curtains, had convertible beds, bathroom, toilet and a private compartment for the owner. The servants were accommodated in a rooftop tent with folding cot beds.

By the early 1930s the Great Depression was having a significant impact on the economies of the USA and Europe, so expensive consumer items such as motorhomes fell out of favour. Their size and speed relative to the trailer caravan did open up a new opportunity, however. As J. Harris Stone put it:

'The chief advantage of a self-contained motor caravan lies mainly in the fact that you can move about quickly and can carry a considerable amount of baggage. Hence such are largely used by societies, political associations, and such-like institutions for propaganda purposes. Also commercial enterprises find the motor caravan convenient for the same reasons.'

The *Illustrated Sporting and Dramatic News*, 17 May 1930

The motorhome's primary use was in effect that of a travelling showroom. Examples of motorhomes used for this and other non-recreational purposes are included in Chapter 8.

The Leyland Terrier motorhome built for the ex-Khedive of Egypt (UK, 1933)

1930-39: The Golden Era of The Caravan

From the late 1920s until the start of the Second World War, caravanning in Britain thrived in something of a golden era. The impact of the Great Depression was severe, particularly in the mining and heavily industrialized communities of the north. In the south of England wealth and leisure time continued to grow however, particularly amongst the lower middle classes. With a growing customer base, British caravans blossomed into hundreds of various shapes and sizes. Makers such as Eccles, Winchester, Car Cruiser and Cheltenham became household names, with mass production and improved materials bringing down prices and, despite some hiccups, improving overall quality. Experimentation continued alongside mass production of the more popular designs. Streamlining became fashionable, even though it was largely irrelevant from a wind resistance viewpoint due to the 30mph speed limit on caravans. By 1936 streamlining was felt by the British caravan press to have been 'overdone', and in the late 1930s designs generally became less rounded and more pragmatic.

As the 1930s progressed, it was clear that caravanners were no longer confining themselves to holidays in summer. Many went caravanning year round and a few even went overseas. More powerful automobiles meant that caravans could be bigger and heavier than before, with the capacity to accommodate ever greater creature comforts. If a full-sized kitchen could come along too, more families could be convinced that this was no longer glorified camping. Caravan construction methods progressed considerably – insulation and materials improved, chassis strength was increased and batteries, electrical lighting and appliances became more sophisticated. But in conservative Britain it helped if the caravan still looked homely – there was little interest in anything that looked externally like a toaster or a silver bullet.

A Car Cruiser caravan in Henley for the RAC Caravan Rally (UK, 1933)

The most significant vehicle design trend of the 1930s was streamlining. Caravans were not immune from the shift toward the curved designs that gave automobiles strong showroom appeal. Aircraft designer and artist C. Fleming-Williams was one of the first British caravan 'streamliners'. His earliest caravan designs used ideas and parts from the aircraft industry. Nicknamed 'Streamline Bill', he established the Car Cruiser company in 1925. He was fascinated by aircraft design and during the war had, like Piggott Bros., noticed the ease with which aircraft trailers could be towed. Fleming-Williams built his first prototype caravan on a De Havilland aircraft axle in 1920 and began production in late 1924. To save space and weight, the caravan's rear end sloped downwards and the beds were placed at the back where maximum headroom was not needed. This was to become a common layout feature of English caravans.

A Car Cruiser caravan (UK, 1936)

The products of the Car Cruiser company became instantly recognisable for their cut-off fronts and sloping backs. The shape came to be known as 'beetle-back'. Early Car Cruiser caravans had single-layer canvas roofs to reduce weight, later replaced by double canvas to reduce condensation. Further innovations made by Fleming-Williams were sloping walls to reduce drag, low profile axles, lightweight body skins and corner-supporting legs. Fleming-Williams' caravans weighed under 1 ton and were reputed to tow easily. The basic design of the 1920 prototype continued with only minor modifications until 1936. Car Cruiser maintained a large hire fleet to help develop familiarity with their caravans.

In 1930, a caravan called the Winchester with a tapered roof and rounded corners appeared on the market. Named after the city in which they were built, Winchester was the new brand name for Bertram Hutchings' caravans, and it revolutionized caravan design in the UK. His streamlined Winchester was based on almost twenty years of caravan building experience. Hutchings shared the view of Fleming-Williams that full-height headroom was not needed along the entire length of a caravan. Most Winchester models of the 1930s had similar styling to the first model of 1930. Winchester caravans became synonymous with quality, elegant lines and good design. As a keen caravanner himself, Hutchings would test his models extensively before sale. By the late 1930s Winchester models such as the 15ft 9in, 2-3 berth caravan had triple insulation in the walls and roof, a bay window, a bureau and an external door for the toilet. Hutchings' caravans remained in much demand as 'the Rolls-Royce of caravans', as company advertising called them, until production ceased in 1959.

Meanwhile, Eccles had smartly established itself as a 'jack of all trades' RV manufacturer during the 1920s until the direction of the immature RV market had become clear. Once the dominance of the trailer caravan had become self-evident, Eccles decided to focus in the decade that followed on making and selling good quality trailer caravans at reasonable prices. Regular advertising, sponsored newspaper articles, strong dealership links and a thriving caravan hire business helped the company to grow the British caravan sector almost single-handedly into a major industry. Eccles also sold overseas – if any British caravan was seen abroad the chances were that it would have an Eccles badge. The Rileys learned that as well as caravan hire, well-publicized domestic and overseas caravan trials in conjunction with the latest model automobiles could build consumer awareness and confidence in the company's products. Eccles would also compete with Winchester at the high end of the caravan market, producing the 18.5ft Eccles Senator in both standard and specially-built versions for wealthy caravanners. It was one of their largest models, incorporating curved lines top and bottom but in a less radical fashion than some competitors.

Above: The first Winchester brand caravan (UK, 1930)

Below: A Winchester 2-3 berth caravan (Europe, 1938)

A Rolls-Royce 40/50 Phantom 1 Barker three-quarter coupe with a specially-built Eccles caravan at Beauly Firth near Inverness, Scotland. The combination was owned by Major and Mrs. H. Martineau – the lady in the photo is probably Mrs Martineau. The photo was taken by renowned Scottish portrait photographer Andrew Paterson (UK, c1938)

British celebrities were often asked by the major manufacturers of the 1930s to promote their caravans. Some agreed, others went even further and bought one. Eccles was particularly successful in achieving good publicity for its products with the help of actresses such as Gracie Fields and Nora Swinburne. Annie Croft and Jean Colin were also photographed by the British press enjoying caravan holidays. These celebrity endorsements were helpful in boosting sales, although not on the same scale as Hollywood stars and their travel trailers from the 1930s onwards.

Like Bertram Hutchings and his new Winchesters, Eccles gradually incorporated streamlining into its caravans. Early Eccles caravans had been highly popular because they had

house-like features, giving tentative customers comfort that they were simply buying or renting a 'house on wheels'. But the company jumped on the streamlining bandwagon in the 1930s with a succession of models that moved away from their more traditional, box-shaped vans.

Mass production at what Eccles claimed in 1935 was 'the largest caravan factory in the world' helped Eccles keep their prices down. Lightweight construction methods allowed Eccles caravans to be pulled by cars with engines as small as 10hp. At its pre-war peak, Eccles was producing fifty caravans a week, allowing caravans such as the Eccles National to be sold for just £125. Eccles continued building caravans into the 1950s. Intense post-war competition led to the company

The Airlite Coronation caravan (UK, 1937)

losing its dominant position however, with their products seen over time as conservative and no longer 'cutting edge'. They were eventually purchased by Sam Alper's Caravans International in 1960.

The use of new materials in the manufacture of caravans in the 1930s contributed to the streamlining process. Clifford Dawtrey, the owner of Airlite Caravans, used his automobile industry experience to produce a number of lightweight caravans in the late 1930s including the Caravan de Luxe in 1936 and the folding Minx in 1937. Airlite used Bakelite, the first synthetic plastic, to round off the corners of some of his models. This technique met with mixed results, however, since the application process was complex and the Bakelite sometimes crazed. But Airlites were

the early predecessors of the plastic and fibreglass caravans that became popular from the 1950s onwards.

In 1938 Airlite Caravans failed. Unperturbed, Dawtrey continued his adventures in new materials with a steel-panelled caravan called the Coventry Steel Phantom Knight. The Phantom Knight incorporated rolled steel panels welded together with an inner wooden frame. The steel made the caravan extremely heavy however, and it was only in production for a year, with the steel being replaced by aluminium. But even this change was not successful, and production was soon discontinued. British consumers had shown a clear distaste for aluminium-built caravans, in sharp contrast to the new models coming out of the USA in the late 1930s.

The Coventry Steel Phantom Knight (UK, 1938)

Above left: Alfred Ensor's caravan with a fold-out rear kitchen. The design was intended to facilitate food preparation without interruption from other occupants but ended up saving little space. A later model with an external toilet was better received (UK, 1935)

Above middle: Ensor's three-wheeled caravan. The front wheel was mounted in motorcycle forks. The merits of towing a caravan with three wheels are questionable (UK, 1936)

Above right: The County caravan's unique feature was a 'sun flap' along one side. Owners apparently found the feature useful, but others thought it made the caravan look like a mobile snack bar (UK, 1936)

Above left: The Rollalong was striking, if somewhat inelegant, for its extending lantern roof and rear entry double door. It had an internal shower and a range of layouts and furniture, allowing customisation by customers (UK, 1936)

Above middle: Bertram Hutchings experimented with a US-styled caravan called the Winchester Wagon, but the design was viewed as 'unhomely' by the British and very few were sold (UK, 1937)

Above right: The Bampton caravan had a double bed which swung out on a horizontal hinge. The Bampton was one of the more successful early extending caravans which were generally plagued with waterproofing and reliability issues (UK, 1937)

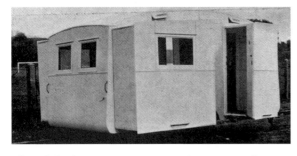

Above left: The Fairway Conway Castle was one early caravan to make use of slide-outs. It had four, two on each side. Slide-outs added weight and complexity to caravans and so came to be used mainly in semi-permanent homes (UK, 1937)

Above middle: The Lolode Trailer Coach was one of the first twin-axle caravans. It was designed by a horsebox manufacturer and was intended to carry passengers. It weighed just under 2 tons (UK, 1937)

Above right: Eccles used their mass production advantages to full effect with the Eccles National. Built in batches of 50, the 14.5ft. National cost a low £125 (UK, 1939)

Experimentation in caravan design continued at a steady pace up to the start of the Second World War. Designs introduced during this period included a twin-axle caravan, a three-wheeled caravan and a number of caravans with slide-out sections designed to increase internal space. Some of these concepts have survived into the modern RV era whilst others have not. A selection of the more interesting ideas appears in the gallery opposite.

By the end of the 1930s, thanks to the efforts of Eccles, Winchester, Car Cruiser and many others, the recreational caravan was no longer an object of curiosity but a common sight on the roads of Britain. It offered one of the most cost-effective ways to spend a week or two at the beach or in the country. Nearly everyone could afford a caravan holiday. The British caravanning boom of the 1930s led to a significant increase in the number of caravan manufacturers. Caravan historian Roger Ellesmere records no less than 177 British caravan makers who were active at some point prior to the Second World War.

By 1939 the British caravan had developed its own unique style. Oval shaped, solid walls and roof, medium-sized and always 'homely' inside with soft furnishings, curtains and small rectangular windows. Experiments with raised roofs, slide-outs and flaps were abandoned in favour of the simple, solid caravan that kept out the cold and could not malfunction in the rain. Caravans made of steel or aluminium were out of the question, whilst camper trailers were left to those with stronger camping instincts or better weather.

As the Second World War approached, sales of all forms of RV slowed considerably. Caravans took on a new role as mobile wartime administration offices or temporary homes for displaced people. The pursuit of leisure was replaced by the need for survival. Nevertheless, through the efforts of a few brave pioneers and a combination of experimentation, design innovation, manufacturing prowess and smart marketing, the foundations had been laid for the strong post-war growth of the British RV market. The country had conceived a new form of leisure that would spread overseas and turn millions worldwide into wanderers.

CHAPTER 3
FRANCE AND BELGIUM

" Comfort, independence, economy - the three requirements of tourism. The caravan has them all.

L' Auto–Vélo, 5 February 1919 "

Opposite: Charles Louvet's *Carling Home No. 1* (France, 1924)

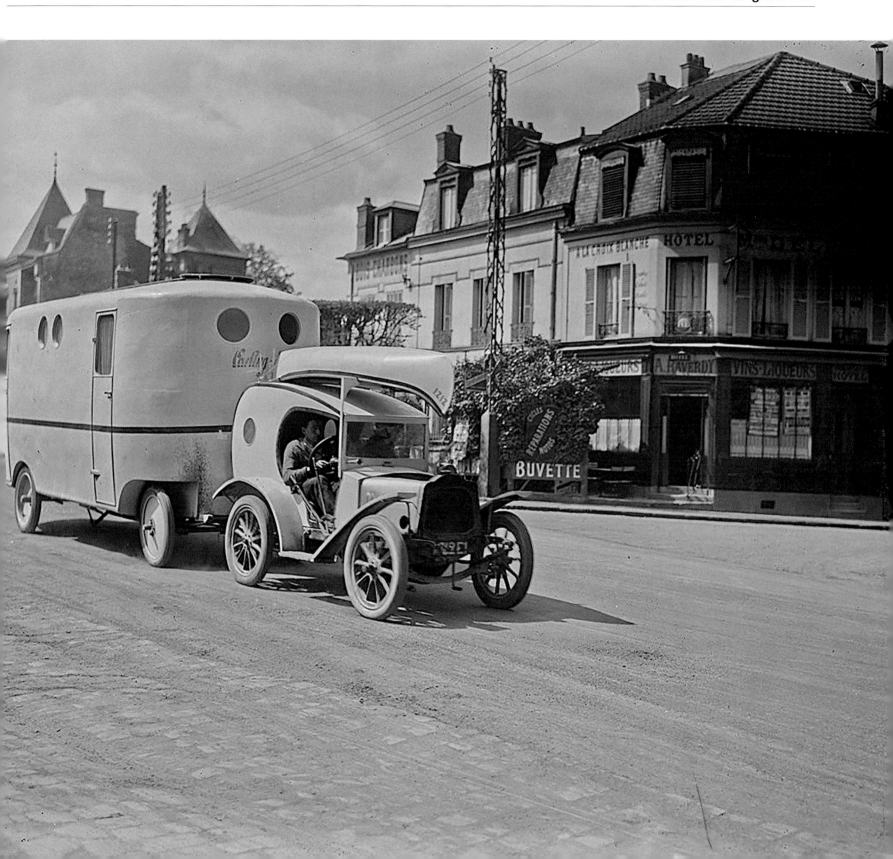

French RV Pioneers before 1900

France's significant contribution to the early development of the RV has been under-reported to date, especially so in the English language. France is pre-eminent in automobile history, with its inventiveness in the field apparent across a wide range of vehicle and propulsion types. It is hardly surprising then, that France was also an early leader in RV design and use.

In late nineteenth-century France, conditions were ideal in three key areas for the swift adoption of motorized transport. First, the country had a well-established and good quality road network developed in Napoleonic times for the rapid deployment of troops to protect the country's extensive land borders. Second, French *carrossiers*, or coachbuilders, were skilled, experienced and flexible. As the traditional horse-drawn carriage declined in popularity, coachbuilders welcomed the opportunity to apply their skills to motorized transport in all its new forms. Third, French government support for industrial innovation was strong, leading to a series of automobile exhibitions and road races between 1895 and 1908 that promoted innovation, increased competition and captured the public's imagination.

French literature may have been another source of inspiration for the country's early RV designers. The possibilities of new and wonderful forms of transport were explored in French science fiction, notably in the novels of Jules Verne. Many are familiar with Captain Nemo's underwater ship *Nautilus* from Verne's 1870 novel *20,000 Leagues Under the Sea* as well as the hot air balloon from *Around the World in Eighty Days*, written in 1872. But Verne's imagination was also land-based. In 1880 he wrote *La Maison à Vapeur* (The Steam House) which featured a mechanical, steam-driven elephant pulling two carriages that were luxurious 'homes on wheels'. So with good roads, good coachbuilders and a supportive government, not to mention a little imagination, France found itself in the late 1800s at the forefront of motor vehicle design. But before the mechanically-powered French RV came its horse-drawn predecessor.

As in Britain, French circus owners were some of the first to use horse-drawn caravans. Circus proprietor and horseman Antonio Franconi was one of the earliest. He was born in Italy but lived in Paris and was described in French and British journals of the early nineteenth century as the inventor of the '*voiture nomade*', or nomadic coach. Franconi's coach was a popular attraction on the streets of Paris during the 1820s and 1830s. According to a report in the *Edinburgh Annual Register* of 1809, Franconi's caravan was 15ft long, drawn by four horses and had hay racks attached to each side which could feed up to twenty horses. The interior was divided into two apartments

From *La Maison à Vapeur* (The Steam House) by Jules Verne (France, 1880)

with a servant's bed suspended between the horse shafts. The vehicle was apparently beautifully decorated.

Much later another circus proprietor, Ernest Molier of Paris, travelled through France by caravan during the summers of 1885 to 1890. He found travelling between towns on public transport uncomfortable and viewed hotels with horror. His caravan consisted of a lounge, two *couchettes*, a kitchen and seating for six on the roof. One or two separate wagons were used to carry tents for people and horses – five or six horses were needed to pull both vehicles. The Molier convoy would travel 30 to 45 kilometres a day and was often mistaken for a family of gypsies.

By the 1890s the caravan habit had begun to spread beyond the circus community. The *Gazette des Eaux* of 21 July 1892 reported that Monsieur Schirrer, a wealthy businessman from Nice, was holidaying that year in Switzerland and Italy with a caravan. The caravan was large and luxuriously appointed, including a lounge, bedroom, kitchen and bathroom. Luggage included a bicycle, an 11-metre demountable boat and hunting and fishing equipment. Drawn by three horses, the caravan could accommodate Schirrer's entire party of eight including the family's servants.

The earliest-known photograph of a French, non-circus recreational caravan is from 1894. Less than a decade after Dr Gordon Stables' trip to Scotland in *The Wanderer*, a wealthy French horseman called Fernand Révil used a horse-drawn caravan to visit England, Holland, Spain, Italy, Greece and Egypt. Révil's interests were broad and included archaeology, architecture and photography. He designed the caravan himself to include two rooms with a small front balcony, large bed, dining table, corner toilet, 60-litre water tank on the roof and a wood-burning stove. The caravan was built by a Monsieur Gagneaux from Lorey, weighed 2,500kg and could travel at 10-12km/h if needed. Révil's travels demonstrate that at the end of the nineteenth century the gentlemen gypsies of England were not alone in Europe in their leisure caravanning pursuits. But French adventurers such as Révil were few and far between. It was not until the advent of motorized vehicles towards the end of the nineteenth century that recreational road travel became more than just the whim of a few intrepid individuals.

Fernand Révil with his wife and their caravan (France, 1894)

Monsieur Levassor's Caravan

Two articles from 1895 contain a description of what may be the world's first leisure caravan towed by a powered vehicle. The concept came from the fertile mind of renowned French automobile engineer Émile Levassor, co-founder of the Panhard Levassor automobile company, shortly before his death in 1897. G. Pierron, in the *Revue Mensuelle du Touring Club de France* of February 1895, described Levassor's caravan as follows:

'Now, would you like to know about the latest thing in automobile locomotion? It is the caravan, which M. Levassor, our delegate for the thirteenth district in Paris, is in the process of building for his own use. It consists of a kind of large wagon with two wheels. Its front end is fitted with an articulated stand and is attached to a petrol tow vehicle by means of a moving boom. Inside is a small kitchen, then a large room with windows that resemble a yacht's lounge, serving simultaneously the purpose of lounge, dining room and bedroom which can sleep six people. At the rear is a small open platform. The weight of this house on wheels is fairly considerable, and the petrol tow vehicle, despite having a 10hp engine, can only just tow it at 15km/h. But would you want to tow it quickly to any particular destination? The caravan can be unhitched and left by the roadside on its stand. The six travellers can then sit in the tow vehicle on

ad hoc seats and, carrying less weight, the tow vehicle can be driven at 28km/h thanks to a special gearbox. Don't you think this is something that cannot be bettered?'

Together with an earlier report of Levassor's caravan in *Le Véloce-Sport* of 10 January 1895, these are the first known references to an unpowered recreational caravan being built for towing by a petrol automobile. Interestingly both articles highlighted what was to become a key advantage of the trailer caravan over the motorhome – the fact that it can be left on site to permit local exploration in the tow vehicle alone.

Unfortunately it is not known if Levassor's caravan was ever finished or, if it was, what happened to it. Intriguingly, there are some similarities between the description of Levassor's caravan and the *Pathfinder* caravan owned by Robert Scase in England around 1906 (see pages 80-81). But any connection between the two must remain entirely speculative until further information comes to light. But what can be said, based on these articles, is that the idea of a motor-drawn leisure caravan was first conceived in France in 1895.

The First Steam-Powered RVs (1896-1900)

The first French powered RVs that were undoubtedly built were steam-drawn. Unlike the gentlemen gypsies of Britain, who did not wish their rural tranquillity to be disrupted by machines, the owners of the first steam-driven French RVs were more interested in owning mobile status symbols. The first two that have been recorded belonged to two Paris-based Russian princes.

In December 1896 the Paris *Salon du Cycle*, or cycle exhibition, included an automobile display. One of the exhibits that attracted much interest was a steam-drawn *Grande Diligence* carriage belonging to Paris-based Prince Oldenburg of Russia.

The tow vehicle was manufactured by De Dion-Bouton, a French engine and motor vehicle manufacturer. It comprised a 30hp steam engine and a 15kg boiler which when loaded with coal weighed 3,200kg. The carriage, made by Fernand Peltier at coachbuilder Carrosserie Industrielle, was divided into two sections: the forward, more elegant part was designed for the owners, whilst the utilitarian rear section was reserved for the servants. The luxury front section was well ventilated, well upholstered and could be converted into a dining room, gaming room or bedroom. In the servants' section there was a wash basin, water closet and trunk containing bedding for the bunk beds. Purpose-built for the prince with long trips over rough roads in the Caucasus in mind, the carriage was equipped with artillery-type wheels, mild steel axles and long

Monsieur and Madame Levassor prior to the start of the Paris-Bordeaux-Paris race (France, 1895)

Above: Louis Poyet's engraving of the *Grande Diligence* of Prince Oldenburg (France, 1896)

Right: A steam-drawn caravan design by Train Scotte, probably for Prince Orloff. Engraving by Louis Poyet (France, 1898)

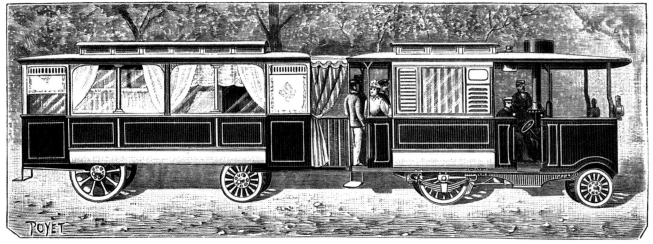

suspension springs. The tow vehicle and carriage combined weighed 5 tonnes and could travel at 30km/h.

In 1897 Prince Vladimir Orloff, the Russian ambassador in Paris, decided to follow the example of Prince Oldenburg and ordered a 'motorized caravan'. Orloff was a patron of the automobile industry, owning the Panhard car that won the 1898 Paris to Amsterdam race. He also helped the Russian royal family to build a large automobile collection. Prince Orloff's vehicle was more ambitious than Oldenburg's – it was longer, heavier and with an articulated central section intended as a 'summer dining room'. Servants were to share space with the steam engine up front, whilst the Prince's rear private compartment was to have a lounge, dining room, three sofa beds, a library and a bathroom.

Prince Orloff's caravan was to be built by Train Scotte, a participant in the *Concours des Poids Lourds*, or heavy vehicle trials, of that year. On 16 April 1898, the periodical *La Nature* includes a drawing and the layout of a steam drawn caravan being built by Train Scotte, and whilst no reference to the prince is made, it was almost certainly his. The weight of the front vehicle including the engine and supplies of fuel and water was estimated at 5.5 tonnes, the rear vehicle weighed 2.5 tonnes in running order, making a total of 8 tonnes. The average expected speed was between 14 and 16km/h.

After this mention, Prince Orloff's steam-driven caravan disappears from view. It was probably never built. It is likely that Prince Orloff's caravan design was over-ambitious and simply too heavy and impractical to be completed. Nevertheless, the prince's ideas alone would have helped to advance prevailing thinking behind the design of early leisure vehicles.

For the earliest-known photo of a steam-powered RV, we have a Parisian resident called Monsieur Rénodier to thank. He was described in the French press as a 'tourist' as well as the 1,000th member of the Automobile Club of France. The newspaper *La Vie au Grand Air* ('Life in the Open Air') writes on 15 May 1898:

'In recent times on the roads of the Bois de Boulogne you may have seen an immense caravan rolling along at the decent speed of 12 to 15km/h. The caravan is 12 metres long and 3 or 4 metres high, painted green and towed by a De Dion tow vehicle of a modest 30hp. It is hard to describe the stupefaction of people who come across this vehicle, which has all the advantages of a normal house but can be moved more easily.

'It comprises a kitchen, a dining room, several bedrooms with real beds and a lounge. In a word, there is nothing lacking in this caravan, either in the apartments or on the upper deck, which can be reached by a small staircase. We should not forget to mention a small Italian terrace where you may get some fresh air and view the best countryside in the world.

'This charming caravan, which has not taken long to find a rich buyer, travels at an average speed of about 18km/h. Its running costs are about 25 cents per kilometre, which is not excessive for a mode of transport if one considers that one can lodge for free along the boulevards, the Champs-Élysées or by the sea.'

Interestingly, an earlier article in a periodical called '*La Revue Générale des Sciences Pures et Appliquées*' ('General Review of Pure and Applied Science') attributes Monsieur Rénodier's

The steam-drawn caravan of Monsieur Rénodier (France, 1897)

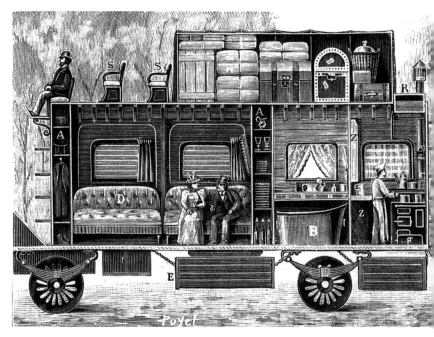

A cutaway engraving of the Rénodier caravan by Louis Poyet (France, 1897)

inspiration for this caravan to the horse-drawn barges of the Thames, which contained lounges, kitchens and beds for overnight stops along the river. This is a further early reference linking the interior design of a caravan to the space-efficient layout found in boats.

La Nature in April 1898 provides some more technical details of the Rénodier caravan. Built by a Parisian coachbuilder called Monsieur Jeantaud, the caravan alone weighed around 4,000kg. All credit must go to Monsieur Rénodier for taking on this challenge, but whether the combined tow vehicle and trailer weight of 7.5 tonnes allowed him to travel far beyond Paris' Bois de Boulogne in the company of his dog is not known.

The number of unusual vehicles designed for recreation in the late 1890s grew slowly in France in the early 1900s. In 1900 we see what is currently thought to be the first ever 'motorhome' in the sense of both propulsion and accommodation being combined in one vehicle. It was again powered by steam and was called the *Quo Vadis*.

Quo Vadis was built by steam and petrol vehicle manufacturer Turgan-Foy & Cie for a trip across Algeria and Tunisia. *Le Journal* of 20 December 1902, with two years of hindsight, is in no doubt of its significance:

'We should remember that the first motorized caravan, Quo Vadis, which brought to life the steam-powered house of Jules Verne, came from the establishment of Turgan-Foy.'

Turgan-Foy were known for their lightweight petrol vehicles that performed well in long-distance road races. They also constructed heavier vehicles for goods and passenger transportation using more powerful steam engines for this purpose. The vehicle later to be named *Quo Vadis* was earlier entered in the omnibus category of the *Concours des Poids Lourds*, or heavy vehicle trials, of October 1900 at Vincennes, winning both the speed and hill climb categories. It was then adapted for long distance travel and, in the process, put on some weight. *Quo Vadis* was usually driven with Monsieur Turgan at the wheel and was powered by two 20hp steam engines. The front section was reserved for the mechanic and a stoker. In the rear there was a 'yacht chamber', toilet, library, large bed and a table.

There was also a 'special machine activating a dynamo' which provided electricity for heating, cooking and lighting. The vehicle reportedly weighed 6.4 tonnes, including 1 tonne of coal, and proceeded at a slow pace when fully loaded. It had to stop regularly for water, so routes were devised as close to rivers as possible. After its return from Tunisia, the vehicle was exhibited in London in May 1901 followed by the Paris Auto Salon of December 1901. In London, the price of the vehicle was estimated at £1,300.

Turgan-Foy's steam omnibus at the heavy vehicle trials in Paris (France, 1900)

Turgan-Foy's *Quo Vadis* in Africa (Tunisia, 1900)

From Steam to Petrol (1902 to 1919)

A motorhome with a truly international flavour caught the attention of the British and French press in 1902. It was called the *Passe Partout*. Sometimes described as the first motorized caravan, it might be more accurately called the first petrol-driven motorhome, coming two years after the steam-powered *Quo Vadis* of 1900. Built in France, the *Passe Partout* started its journey from London with the rather immodest aim of travelling the world. A British newspaper of the time was highly sceptical of this goal:

'I would be sorry to damp the enthusiasm of this ardent quartet, but, were I a betting man, I would lay a thousand to a hundred it can't be done. And, on the matter of roads, I probably know more about them in Russia, Siberia, China and America than the average wheelman. For thousands of miles they are rather like the often-quoted snakes in Iceland - there ain't none. The "Passe Partout" won't get to the Urals, far less China.'

The Sketch, 23 April 1902

A colourful character called Dr E.E. Lehwess, a British national with a German background, was the owner of the vehicle. One of his many ambitious objectives for the trip was improved Anglo-Russian relations. Using a Panhard Levassor chassis and coachwork by Carrosserie Industrielle, the *Passe Partout*

The French *Passe Partout* in London before its attempted world tour (UK, 1902)

cost £3,000. The engine was Panhard's *Centaure* type with four cylinders generating 30hp. The use of an internal combustion engine offered significant weight benefits over steam – *Passe Partout* weighed 'only' 3 tonnes fully loaded. The scepticism of the British press proved well founded when the *Passe-Partout* ground to a halt in the Russian countryside outside St Petersburg. The vehicle was abandoned there by Dr Lehwess but was later returned to the UK and placed on exhibition.

France's early lead in the development of 'motor caravans' was starting to receive attention across the channel in England. A British newspaper of 1903 reported rather angrily:

'The latest thing in the automobile world is a motor caravan, which has been constructed for touring purposes for a member of a Bordeaux club. The idea has long been talked about but it has been left to the Frenchmen, as usual, to lead the way.'

The Manchester Courier and Lancashire General Advertiser,
14 October 1903

The motorhome in question was *La Bourlinguette*, built in the south of France. There is no formal word *bourlinguette* in the French language, but *bourlinguer* means to roam or wander, so the name of this motorhome could have been something of a homage to Gordon Stables' 1885 caravan, *The Wanderer*.

Built for Jules Secrestat, son of a wealthy Bordeaux industrialist and a keen automobile enthusiast, by local coachbuilder Monsieur Henri Lafitte, *La Bourlinguette* was built to high standards of luxury. The 20hp Panhard Levassor petrol engine and 15-18km/h average speed was less of a highlight than the interior, which was divided into three rooms: a mechanic's room at the front with driving seats and a folding bed; a large room in the centre that could be used as a lounge, dining room or bedroom; and a kitchen and office at the rear. *La Bourlinguette* weighed 3 tonnes and included a number of measures to reduce noise and vibration including soft carpets, thick curtains, slipper brakes, soft spring suspension and 'special devices' to stop rattles. It was a far cry from the utilitarian motorhomes of Dr Lehwess and Turgan-Foy.

In the early 1900s as automobiles became more powerful and more reliable, France's leading automobile manufacturers began

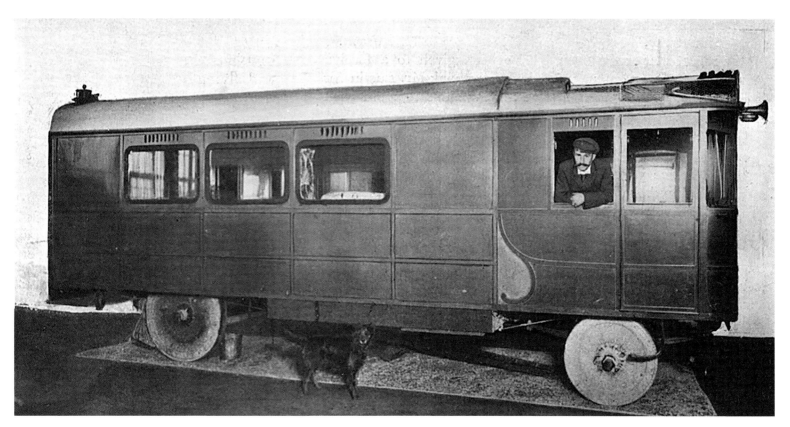

La Bourlinguette (France, 1903)

De Dietrich's *Voiture de Route* (Germany, c1906)

to explore the long-distance travel potential of their vehicles. In 1904, as an alternative to the towed caravan or motorhome, a new type of recreational vehicle appeared. It was De Dietrich's 40hp *Voiture de Route* or touring car. It was a luxurious, long-wheelbase limousine with a large internal area for seating and occasional sleeping. It first appeared in Paris at the Automobile Salon in December 1904 followed by the Olympia Motor Show in London in February 1905 and Berlin in 1906. Promoted in London as the Great Touring Saloon or Grand Pullman, the

French press called it the '*Domomobile*'. There were big queues in both London and Paris to see this long-distance tourer. De Dietrich used their railway coachbuilding experience to create a luxury interior similar to that of first class railway carriages of the day. According to the UK's *Bystander* of 8 February 1905:

'The front section is fitted with four armchairs, which are so arranged that the whole thing can be converted into a comfortable sleeping saloon, with two beds. Folding tables, writing desks, a revolver case and a medicine chest are only some of this car's features. It should appeal to those on the look out for a cheap flat!'

The reason for the revolver case is unknown, but clearly the manufacturers expected owners to travel into parts of the world that required such precautions. De Dietrich's touring car concept was adopted by a number of other manufacturers both in France and internationally over the next decade. For example, Welch and Pierce-Arrow of the USA produced touring limousines in 1909 and 1910 respectively (see pages 112-113). Luggage racks were often added at the rear or on the roof for long-distance travel. Touring cars were novel but affordable only by the wealthy. Sleeping inside the vehicle would have been contemplated only if a suitable hotel along the way could not be found.

The more powerful engines that led to the development of the touring car also supported the construction of larger caravans and motorhomes. In 1906 a French nobleman called Baron de Sennevoy made a big splash in Paris with his gigantic *Comet* caravan. Although the *Comet* was reported in 1910 to have been towed by an 18hp *tracteur* (motorized tow vehicle), as far as we know it was only ever photographed with three horses pulling its 6 tonnes. It was built to allow the Baron and Baroness to pursue a Bohemian lifestyle. It included a removable balustrade along with a servants' entry at the front, a folding toilet, a piano, organ, telephone and 90-gallon water tank. It was possibly one of the first ever insulated caravans, felt being used to line the double-panelled walls to reduce noise and insulate against the cold.

Previously in 1905 Baron de Sennevoy had formed an organisation called the House Car Club to promote the construction and enjoyment of caravans. Some 600 guests were invited to its inaugural meeting – a discussion of the organisation's purpose was put off to a future meeting and everyone was invited to a celebration instead. It is not known how long the organisation survived.

The Comet in Paris (France, c1908)

A Mystery Caravan

In 2014 a mysterious caravan surfaced in online photography archives described only as a 'Panhard Levassor car and caravan, 1900s, England'. It is potentially significant because it shows one of the earliest petrol-drawn caravans ever made.

The car has been verified with the Panhard et Levassor Club GB as being from around 1900, with a UK registration plate around 1906. The caravan's origin is unknown but is probably French.

It contains some unique features including a third wheel at the front, French-style bodywork, a roof rack and double doors. The windows and roller blinds are reminiscent of a railway carriage or omnibus. The photo was probably taken in the north of England in the early 1900s. So, what was a French caravan doing in England?

J. Harris Stone, the first secretary of the UK Caravan Club, gives us a clue. His 1914 book *Caravanning and Camping Out* contains a description of a three-wheeled caravan which is remarkably close to the one in the photograph:

Panhard Levassor car and caravan (UK, early 1900s)

The First Rooftop Camper

French innovation in recreational vehicles was exemplified in 1906 with the development of a rooftop camping vehicle, likely to be the world's first. Developed by Monsieur Amagoris and mounted on a 40hp chassis, it contained sleeping and cooking facilities, a ladder, ice box and even a wine cellar. Described by *La Vie au Grand Air* as unsuitable for winter use, it was an unusual configuration that would have suited only those with no fear of heights.

The rooftop camping vehicle of Monsieur Amagoris (France, 1906)

'The caravan "Pathfinder" is in several respects unusual, if not quite unique. In the first place it runs on three wheels only, and is easily drawn by one horse. The main door to the saloon is at the rear, and there is besides, near the front on the near side, a "kitchen entrance" as Mr Robert A. Scase, the owner, calls it – formed of double doors which open square.'

The book continues to describe other features of Scase's caravan that are remarkably similar to those shown in the photograph. The complication of course is that Harris Stone describes this caravan as being horse-drawn. Angela Willis, curator of the UK's Caravan and Motorhome Club archives, has a possible

answer to this riddle. She believes Scase may have abandoned the motor vehicle and substituted it for a horse due to the impracticalities of towing a coach-built caravan with an underpowered automobile on the poor roads of the day.

Scase is known to have lived in Derbyshire in northern England, founding the Derbyshire Village Mission in 1916 and preaching the gospel in local villages in a horse-drawn caravan. It is possible that as a member of a wealthy property-owning family of Surbiton near London, he purchased the car and caravan as a package at a motor show or exhibition prior to moving to Derbyshire. Research on this mystery caravan continues.

Hybrids and Conversions

During the second decade of the twentieth century, French experimentation with RV design continued. With no textbook to follow, manufacturers were free to blur the lines between motorhomes and caravans. In 1913 an interesting hybrid RV appeared in the form of a motorhome towing an unpowered trailer caravan. The *Revue Mensuelle du Touring Club de France* published an article by the owner of this unusual combination called Monsieur Bouthet des Gennetières, a self-described 'avid tourist'. The hybrid RV was called *Le Rêve*, or *The Dream*.

Initially used as a single horse-drawn trailer from about 1905, the trailer was later hitched to the back of a motorhome in about 1911. An engine was introduced to overcome the problem of stabling four horses each night. The motorhome was a converted truck with a 22hp engine and weighed 2,500kg. The trailer caravan weighed 2,230kg and was built by Felix Veillat of Coulon. With his wife, three children and servants, Bouthet des Gennetières travelled extensively throughout France at speeds up to 25km/h at a cost of around 25 francs per day, some 40 francs less than staying at a hotel. He exhorted his compatriots to travel more extensively in this way. But with a total weight of some 4.7 tonnes, this combination would have been suitable for well-paved roads only.

A smaller, faster and altogether more light-hearted RV appeared in 1912. The self-named *Menagerie Grégoire* was a 3-ton Grégoire vehicle adapted to carry driver Jean Porporato and eleven passengers on the San Sebastian Rally of 1912. The car began the rally in Posen, Germany (now Poznań in Poland) and won the race, which took account of weight and distance covered rather than just speed, completing the 3,500km journey in about seven days. The vehicle came complete with flower boxes, broomsticks and a bird cage. Although mildly eccentric, this RV demonstrated that automobiles could be adapted for leisure use and travel successfully over long distances.

Le Rêve motorhome and caravan (France, c1911)

La Menagerie Grégoire (France, 1912)

A Belgian Fifth Wheeler

The 'fifth wheel' luxury motorhome built for Baron Crawhez (France, 1913)

The interior of Baron Crawhez's motorhome (France, 1913)

A short diversion to Belgium is necessary in this chapter to describe an important pre-war RV made for a baron. Its importance lies in the fact that it was one of the earliest petrol-driven 'fifth wheelers' ever built. A fifth wheeler's hitch sits above rather than behind the rear axle of the tow vehicle, reducing turning circle diameter and, more importantly, improving towing stability. Baron Pierre de Crawhez was a pioneering Belgian racing driver, establishing one of the earliest closed circuit races in Belgium in the Ardennes in 1902. Between 1912 and 1913, based on a concept of his elder brother Jean, he commissioned an Auto Salon de Luxe recreational vehicle for a hunting trip to Morocco and Algeria. This was a significant upgrade to his earlier, somewhat ramshackle hunting vehicle of 1909. The tow vehicle or *tracteur* of his fifth-wheeler successor was a 30hp Auto-Mixte Pescatore. Auto-Mixte was a Belgian company that built vehicles using the hybrid gasoline-electric technology of inventor Henri Pieper. The rear coach was built by Belgian coachbuilder Vogt and De Meuse from Liège.

The combined tow vehicle and coach was massive, weighing 5 tonnes and measuring 10.5m end to end. The interior was elegant without being ostentatious. It included four convertible beds, a separate bed for the chauffeur, lantern roof, electric stove, electric lighting, wine cellar and toilet. According to historian Patrick Robertson, the sale of this vehicle to the Baron fell through for reasons unknown. Consequently, the builders, Auto-Mixte, hired out the vehicle after the First World War to people wishing to tour the battlefields of Flanders. In the process, Auto-Mixte's fifth wheeler became by chance one of the earliest motorized RVs available for hire.

Post-War Recovery

Non-essential manufacturing paused in France during the First World War, after which the automobile industry understandably took some time to recover. The first attempt to revive the nascent French RV industry was driven not by leisure but by the need to provide urgent post-war housing.

A strange vehicle appeared on the streets of Paris one foggy day in November 1920. It was the Cadel collapsible caravan, made by a Parisian trailer manufacturer, Monsieur O. Cadel, who named it the *maison liberée*, or liberated house. Little is known about Cadel's trailer business, except that he produced various types of trailers for the French army during the First World War as well as 'tourism trailers' that were essentially small, open-topped *char à bancs* (see page 22). The *maison liberée* was manufactured to help relieve the post-war housing shortage in the liberated areas of Europe, but its maker hoped it might also come to be used by tourists.

It consisted of two levels, with a bedroom and library upstairs and a saloon, dining room and kitchen on the lower level. The two levels were connected by a wooden staircase. The height of the caravan was reduced from 15ft to 9.5ft when the roof was lowered. Similar technology was used in Britain by caravan makers Shadow and Eccles for their much smaller collapsible caravans of the mid to late 1920s (see pages 47-48). Caravan historian W.M. Whiteman speculated in 1973 that Cadel's caravan may have been built for French wartime needs, but as we now know, it was post-war housing requirements that inspired Cadel's double-decker. A number of Cadel's caravans were ordered by the French government for use in war-damaged regions, but it is not known how many were used for this purpose or indeed for tourism.

A Cadel collapsible caravan turned up much later across the channel in England at the 1938 Caravan Club National Rally. It was owned by a Wing Commander Waller who had brought it in France. What the British thought of Cadel's concept is not known but judging by the guy rope being attached to the vehicle's roof, the Cadel caravan's lack of stability in the face of strong British winds may have been one downside of using this tall caravan in the UK.

The Cadel caravan on the streets of Paris (France, 1920)

The Cadel collapsible caravan owned by Wing Commander W. Waller making an appearance at the 1938 Caravan Club National Rally in Warwick, England (UK, 1938)

During the 1920s France was not ready to build caravans in large numbers – there was simply not enough demand. French journalists reported on caravan developments across the water in Britain but speculated that the French were too afraid of being labelled gypsies or circus folk to take up caravanning as a hobby. The only progress made in the French RV sector during this decade was made by a few enterprising individuals.

Baudry de Saunier was one such person. He was a well-known cycling and automobile journalist and created two important pre-war publications, *La Vie Automobile* and *Omnia*. After the First World War he became editor-in-chief of the *Revue Mensuelle du Touring Club de France*, where he promoted the benefits of tourism and in particular the advantages of travelling by caravan. In 1937 he wrote a book called *Le Camping Pratique Pour Tous (Practical Camping for All)*.

The *Pigeon Vole* caravan of Baudry de Saunier (France, 1924)

De Saunier did not just write about caravans, he also built and used them. Having ordered a 'small, strong two-wheeled caravan' from coachbuilders Rothschild in his early caravanning days, de Saunier went on to build his own caravan in 1922 called the *Pigeon Vole* (The Flying Pigeon, also the name of a children's game in France). *Pigeon Vole* took about forty days to build. It was box-shaped with a gabled 'pop-top' roof. It accommodated up to four people.

De Saunier's knowledge of automobiles led him to design a caravan that did not place undue stress on the tow vehicle when towing. It was a study in light weight and compact design, weighing about 900kg fully laden. Yet it still managed to contain beds, tables, cupboards, stove and fold-out walls for good ventilation. There was even space outside for window boxes full of tulips. The caravan covered long distances during its time. De Saunier wrote extensively about his travels and in doing so helped to promote caravanning in France. He later wondered why caravanning was not more popular. His own theory was that the French were too reluctant to leave their comfortable homes. It was not until the mid to late 1930s that leisure caravans gained broad acceptance.

French motorhomes were few and far between in the 1920s. One that did see the light of day was purchased by a French poet, Raymond Roussel. It was built in 1925 by George Régis and designed by an unknown English engineer. Its weight is not known but it was 30ft long and 7ft wide. It had a sumptuous interior including full-length bath, bedroom, lounge, kitchen and staff quarters. According to one account it was built 'to avoid hotels and the annoyance of service that was often below what he was accustomed to'. Roussel took the motorhome twice around Europe, and whilst in Rome it is reported that he met with both Mussolini and an emissary of the Pope. What these men thought of the motorhome is unknown. It was reported in the press in 1933 that the motorhome had suffered an ignominious fate, having had its roof sliced off whilst going under a bridge. Designing a motorhome to deal with such eventualities was clearly not a high priority in 1925.

At the other end of the weight scale from Roussel's large motorhome was an unusual combination unlikely to be decapitated by a bridge. The *Vélocar* was a four-wheeled recumbent bicycle developed by Charles Mochet from about 1924. It was photographed towing a small caravan in 1925 with Mochet in the driving seat. The caravan may have been designed for use by children. The *Vélocar* was light weight and low cost, appealing to post-war families who could not afford motorized transport. Mochet went on to develop a number of variants of the *Vélocar* including three-wheelers and a motorized version.

The motorhome of poet Raymond Roussel (France, 1925)

Charles Mochet with his *Vélocar* and caravan (France, 1925)

The RVs of Charles Louvet

During the 1920s, one French RV designer stands head and shoulders above all others – Charles Louvet. Louvet single-handedly pushed French RV design towards greater use of lightweight materials and streamlined design as used in the aircraft industry. He brought his innovative ideas to life in a wide range of ground-breaking RV designs, including what is probably the world's first coach-built motorhome (where a body encloses the engine) built between 1923 and 1925. Although all of Louvet's RVs were, as far as we know, one-off prototypes that did not go into production, they were widely exhibited in southern France and would have inspired many other builders and owners to follow the RV lifestyle.

According to Louvet historian Gilles Fillaud, Louvet was the son of an aviation mechanic. At the age of 17 he built a model aeroplane and soon after began building lightweight canoes and rowing boats that he would hire out to the public on the beaches of northern France. His caravan-building career probably began by building a simple wooden caravan to support his canoe construction and rental business and accommodate his family whilst away from home. Caravan building was in the family – Louvet's brother Marcel also built at least one caravan and may have inspired Charles to do likewise.

For health reasons, Charles Louvet moved to Nice in the south of France. It is here that he built his best-known RVs. Between 1921 and 1934 with only the help of his family, he built four RVs using the name *Carling Home* (*carlingue* is the French word for an aircraft cabin) and numbered them from One to Four. Instead of patenting his designs, Louvet would publicly exhibit each RV, charging an entry fee to fund his other inventions. It was reported that Louvet had over fifty inventions to his name including folding canoes, folding bicycles, a pedal car and a range of specialized machines and tools. His canoes were often carried on the roof of his RV or tow vehicle. His coach-built motorhomes featured internal corridors along their length with a door at each end to facilitate paying guests. Louvet would travel

Charles Louvet with his models of a plane and *Carling Home No. 4* (France, date unknown)

A caravan built by Charles Louvet's brother Marcel (France, date unknown)

extensively through France to promote his unusual vehicles to the press and an astounded public. His supportive family would sit in a local café, sometimes late into the night, whilst their mobile home was being exhibited.

His four best-known RVs were as follows:

Carling Home No. 1, built in 1921, was a car and four-wheeled caravan combination. The De Dion tow-vehicle's bodywork was designed and built by Louvet to match the caravan. The tow vehicle also carried a Louvet-built canoe on its roof. Fillaud believes this caravan may have been later sold to French singer and accordion player Paula Chabran.

Carling Home No. 2, built between 1923 and 1925, was what would be called a motorhome today. Some 36ft long and weighing 2 tonnes, it was still much lighter than any other motorhome of a similar size built up to that

date. It is the first known 'coach-built' motorhome, with propulsion and accommodation enveloped in a single, purpose-built body.

Carling Home Sport Louvet No. 3, built in 1929, was a motorhome modified from *Carling Home No. 2,* with triangular side windows and carrying a long canoe on the roof. It was designed to be shorter and therefore more manoeuvrable than *Carling Home No. 2.*

Carling Home No. 4, completed in 1934, was an extremely ambitious caravan design with extending front and rear sections. It measured 11m long when on tow and 18m when extended at rest. Due to its phenomenal length when extended, it did not gain favour in tourism circles but was sold in 1936 or 1937 for use as a commercial display and exhibition caravan. It was used for this purpose into the late 1940s.

Carling Home No. 1 in the south of France (France, date unknown)

Above: *Carling Home No. 2* (France, 1923-25)

Below: *Carling Home Sport Louvet No. 3* (France, 1929)

Above: *Carling Home No. 4* in compact mode (France, 1934)

Below: *Carling Home No. 4* in extended mode (France, 1934)

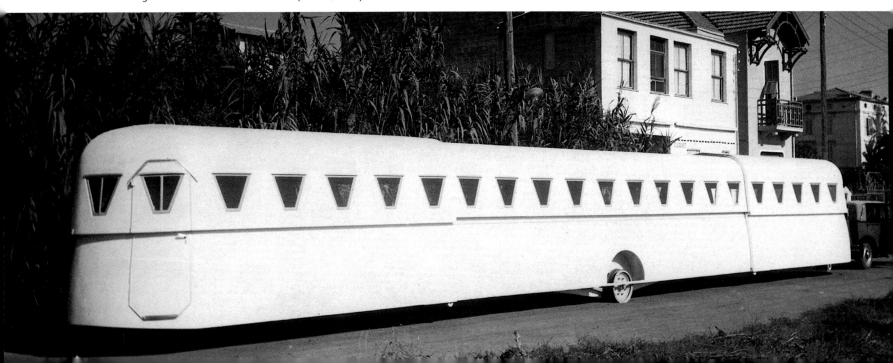

Interior photos of *Carling Home No. 1* show that Charles Louvet may have also designed his own lightweight but attractive furniture, including perforated tables and chairs. Similar chairs were used for Louvet's canoes. These were a good example of form following function and stood in stark contrast to the heavy, domestic furniture used in other truck-based RVs of the period.

The photo of the interior of *Carling Home No.4* (overleaf) shows three RV models being exhibited to visitors. The model at the front, dubbed *Project 1930* by Louvet, is not known to have been constructed. It was of a twin-axle articulated vehicle, probably intended for recreational purposes, and may have been an early design concept for *Carling Home No. 4*. Louvet was clearly seeking a suitable design compromise between space and navigability, but the articulated vehicle would have been complex to build at full scale. If Louvet's creative mind could have been partnered at the time with an automobile engineer, there would almost certainly have been no shortage of fascinating RVs designed by Louvet on the roads of France in the 1930s and beyond.

Above: *Carling Home No. 1* interior and furniture (France, date unknown)

Below: The central section of *Carling Home No. 4* under construction (France, c1933)

Louvet and his family inside *Carling Home No.4* (France, c1934)

Is this a Louvet?

A single photograph exists that was taken in Paris of another motorhome from 1928, the *Home Mobile E*. The motorhome was apparently owned by a couple from Monaco who were touring through France. The *Home Mobile E* is similar in size and shape to *Carling Home Sport Louvet No. 3*, although the art deco-inspired diamond exterior and windows are not in the style of Louvet's other RVs. Although Monaco was close to Louvet's base in the city of Nice, whether he was involved in the design of this RV remains a mystery.

The *Home Mobile E* (France, 1928)

French Caravans of the 1930s

After 1930, the caravan finally became more visible on French roads. As in the UK, the flexibility and affordability of the caravan gave it an advantage over the motorhome. It was not seen in the same numbers as the USA and the UK, but it held a niche position in the leisure market as a comfortable way to enjoy the outdoors. A small number of caravan makers became active in France during the 1930s. Designs varied according to the background and experience of each manufacturer, but the most common design was a mid-sized, oval-shaped caravan with low ground clearance suitable for long-distance touring on France's good roads. A company called Stella produced caravans similar to British designs, but most other manufacturers came up with their own designs.

Notin is perhaps France's best-known manufacturer of the period, followed by Hénon and Rex. Smaller makers such as Georges Lemarié built caravans in low numbers including an unusual caravan called *L'Escargot*, or *The Snail*. French caravans of this period are still carefully collected and restored by a passionate group of RV enthusiasts to this day.

According to French RV historian Bruno Leroux, Francis Notin began constructing horse-drawn fair caravans in 1921 with his younger brother Joseph as an employee. In 1928, both brothers began to build motor-drawn caravans. In 1933, the Notin brothers built a touring caravan for a lawyer from Nice, which deviated from their traditional style by incorporating a side door, skylight, lights and fans. It also contained a library of over 100 books. In 1934, Joseph Notin bought out his brother Francis (who used the proceeds to buy two cinemas) and focused on building touring caravans. In either 1934 or 1935 Notin became the first company to exhibit caravans at the Paris Fair. They were easily recognisable due to their rounded form, barrel-shaped walls, sliding windows and roller blinds. After the Second World War the company continued to build a range of high-quality caravans for frequent travellers. Notin later built a small number of motorhomes based on Renault chassis. Despite falling into bankruptcy in the 1970s, the company revived by specialising in luxury motorhomes.

Descended from a Somme-based family of carpenters and cabinet makers, Henry Hénon built his first caravan for his wife in 1928. The company's goal was simple – to make camping comfortable. This clear motto appealed first to local dignitaries who bought his caravans, and later to visitors at the Paris and Lille Fairs. Serious production commenced in 1934. Hénon reportedly sold 44 caravans between then and the start of the Second World War. Construction methods were similar to those used in aviation, including cotton fabric glued on a wooden frame. The Grand Luxe model of 1938 included a distinctive 'pinched nose' front and oval windows – standard models had square windows. The company continued building caravans until 1972.

Coachbuilder Georges Lemarié built his first caravan for a family member in 1936. The design brief was for a lightweight caravan that could be towed by a low-powered automobile, a rounded front and pointed, streamlined rear. A small, plane-like vertical tail was added by Lemarié at the rear, supposedly for extra lateral stability. The tail disguised an awning locker below. The caravan looked like a shell – and so *L'Escargot* (*The Snail*) was born.

In addition to this small caravan, Lemarié produced a number of other caravan models. He found clever ways to raise the roof for fresh air ventilation, gear systems to transform dining seats into beds and incorporated full-sized toilets.

A Notin caravan (France, c1930s)

A Hénon caravan (France, c1930s)

Georges Lemarié's *L'Escargot* (France, 1936)

The names of his models were based on Parisian landmarks such as Champs-Élysées, Moulin Rouge and Folies Bergère. Lemarié continued to build caravans until his death in the 1960s. Whilst most of his caravan styles were more conventional than *L'Escargot*, they never exceeded 4 metres in length and about 1 tonne in weight. Like many of his predecessors, Lemarié always believed in simple camping, and that it should never be necessary to carry all the accoutrements of home on a caravan holiday.

A keen outdoorsman from America named R.R. Miller came to France during the First World War and decided to stay.

Miller would follow in the footsteps of Baudry de Saunier as an important ambassador for the RV lifestyle. According to French RV historian Pierre-François Dupond, Miller established several camping supply stores in Paris as well as the *Centre Franco-Américain pour L'Auto-Camping* (the French-American Auto Camping Centre). In 1924 Miller wrote a book called *L'Auto Camping,* in which he espoused the low cost and health benefits of automobile camping. Although his efforts to promote the hobby in France met with some success, during the 1930s Miller could see the RV market was heading in a different direction and moved into the caravan business. He established

A Rex two-door caravan (France, late 1930s)

the Rex brand of caravans as well as importing British caravans including models made by Essex, Raven and Car Cruiser.

Caravanes Rex was a Paris-based caravan builder that produced a range of models to suit different tow vehicles and budgets. At least four models are known to have been produced before 1939. Their 1937 catalogue included a 4-berth, 4.48 metre, 500kg Caravane Rex, a similar-sized but heavier (600kg) Caravane Rex Luxe which included a lantern roof and chemical toilet, and a smaller, 3.66 metre 2-berth model suitable for tow vehicles of 8hp or more. The smallest Rex was only 3 metres long and weighed only 330kg when empty, but according to the manufacturers still had everything you could possibly want for your 'home on wheels'. It was suitable for tow vehicles of

7hp or more. Rex suggested their caravans were suitable for business or pleasure, but events overtook the company and it did not survive beyond the Second World War.

All non-essential manufacturing would cease during the Second World War, but most caravan manufacturers resumed production in response to growing post-war demand for affordable holidays in France. Today the caravan and motorhome sit comfortably alongside each other in a country that loves the freedom offered by the RV but is not always fully aware of its rich RV heritage. France's national motto, *'Liberté, Egalité, Fraternité'* ('liberty, equality, fraternity') is equally applicable to the spirit in which RVs are enjoyed throughout the country and could be a worthy motto for users of RVs worldwide.

The Rex sales yard near Paris (France, late 1930s)

CHAPTER 4

UNITED STATES OF AMERICA

" A... reason why I visit the Adirondacks, and urge others to do so, is because I deem the excursion eminently adapted to restore impaired health. Indeed, it is marvellous what benefit physically is often derived from a trip of a few weeks to these woods. To such as are afflicted with that dire parent of ills, dyspepsia, or have lurking in their system consumptive tendencies, I most earnestly recommend a month's experience among the pines. **"**

from *Adventures in the Wilderness; or Camp–Life in the Adirondacks*
by William H.H. Murray (1869)

Opposite: A promotional photo for a Covered Wagon travel trailer (USA, 1938)

The Gilded Age (1870-1900)

Very little has been written about America's RV history before 1910. This is somewhat surprising for a country with such a strong RV heritage and good historical records. The country's horse-drawn RV era is an important one and provides useful clues to the design and use of early American RVs. To tell the full story of the American RV, we need to start in the nineteenth century.

America's so-called 'Gilded Age' from 1870 to 1900 brought about massive industrial and economic change. New roads and railroads were built, an oil and mining boom took place and there was intense urbanisation of America's east coast. Over 27 million Europeans emigrated to the United States between 1865 and 1918 in search of employment and a better quality of life. The new migrants brought with them optimism and ideas. There was an unprecedented wave of industrial creativity, with over half a million patents issued between 1860 and 1890. This economic activity created a new middle class with time, money and a sense of adventure.

Health Seekers and Sheep Herders

The dramatic increase in America's population in the second half of the nineteenth century had a major downside – sickness. Tuberculosis, or consumption, was the leading cause of death in 1850s America and was rife among the crowded, polluted and poorly-sanitized towns and cities of the eastern seaboard. Between 1840 and 1900, thousands of migrants afflicted with tuberculosis and other diseases headed west at the suggestion of their family physician to find the only known 'cure' of the time, a healthier climate and less stressful lifestyle. These people were known as 'health seekers'. So what do these health seekers have to do with the history of the RV? Well, to reach their destinations, health-seekers used horse-drawn vehicles that were the predecessors of the modern American RV.

Unlike Britain, America did not have gypsy wagons as a reference point for the design of their horse-drawn leisure vehicles. Although some European gypsies settled in America from the 1850s onwards, bringing their culture and occasionally their *vardo* wagons with them (the Long Island Museum has a fine example from c1860-1885), they did so in small numbers.

The covered wagons used by America's settlers, explorers and gold diggers are sometimes cited as the early predecessors of the American RV. But this notion is closer to romance than reality. Most animal-drawn vehicles of the settlers were used to transport personal belongings, with their owners sleeping alongside their wagons in tents or under the stars. The Conestoga wagon, for example, was durable but heavy. It carried mainly goods, had no suspension and a curved floor to keep goods from falling out, so would have been highly uncomfortable for any passengers. The lighter bow wagon nicknamed the 'prairie schooner' was used extensively along the settlement trails but was predominantly a goods carrier packed to its canvas roof with the family furniture, leaving nowhere to sleep. Tents and bedrolls were carried on these wagons but taken out for sleeping on the ground at camp. New European settlers may have had their first taste of camping in the company of a covered wagon, but very few will have used one specifically as mobile accommodation or for recreational purposes.

Instead, the first American horse-drawn vehicle designed to allow sleeping along a rough trail was the ambulance wagon. It was box-shaped and had soft springs, reclining or removable seats and rear-loading, flat floors to carry wounded soldiers away from the battlefield. Although a number of two- and four-wheeled ambulance wagon designs were tested during the American Civil War of 1861-1865, ambulance wagons had been in existence well before then. The first US examples were based on the French *ambulance volante* or flying ambulance, first used in 1793 and later employed in conflicts worldwide.

Beyond the field of battle, it was the health seekers who found a new civilian use for the ambulance wagon – as a way to travel long distances in relative comfort. It was the least bone-jarring wagon available at the time and so could be used to help eastern health seekers reach the fresh air of the forests, mountains and lakes to the west. Designed for sleeping or resting on the move, the ambulance wagon also eliminated some of the discomforts of sleeping when halted. It afforded rest and provided shelter without having to erect and dismantle a tent each night. When a major destination had been reached, the comforts offered by the ambulance wagon meant that it was often used for local camping trips.

Convoys of generally healthy settlers would sometimes include an ambulance wagon to carry the more vulnerable members of the group. In 1856 for example, health seeker James Ross Larkin from St. Louis, Missouri purchased for the not inconsiderable sum of $202 an ambulance wagon from local coachbuilders Finlay & Doherty for use along the Santa Fe Trail. Later in 1875, the *Nebraska State Journal* of 12 November 1875 interviewed an 'invalid' English gentleman from North Devon, James K. Newcombe. Newcombe was travelling through

A Zouave (French North African) ambulance crew demonstrating removal of wounded soldiers during the American Civil War using an ambulance wagon (USA, 1860-1865)

Nebraska in a vehicle procured in Toronto, Canada, that may have been a converted ambulance wagon. It was described as a 'roomy, comfortable, covered conveyance, bedroom and kitchen in one, with a little cooking stove and glazed windows and a due complement of carriage lamps'. He travelled 'in search of health and the pleasures which attend health' and went 'as the Quakers worship - when the spirit moves him'. Newspaper reports of similar wagons used for health trips continue through the 1880s.

For hardier souls or for those who could not afford an ambulance wagon, converted farm wagons and surplus US army escort wagons were adapted for camping purposes. These were especially popular with hunters. Although less comfortable

Above: A sheep herder with his wagon in Montana (USA, date unknown)

Opposite: Timothy H. O'Sullivan's wagon in the sand dunes of Carson Desert, Nevada (USA, 1867)

than the ambulance wagon, these used the same box shape and flat floors that better suited mobile accommodation when compared to bow wagons. Nearly all were self-built, some were surprisingly luxurious. A few covered vast distances.

The ambulance wagon was adapted to other uses that also required cautious travel. In 1867, following in the footsteps of British photographer Roger Fenton (see page 18), American Civil War and landscape photographer Timothy O'Sullivan bought an army surplus ambulance wagon to serve as his travelling darkroom during Clarence King's geological exploration of the Fortieth Parallel. The vehicle's soft suspension helped protect O'Sullivan's fragile photographic equipment.

Another vehicle that influenced early American RV design was the sheep herder's wagon. This was a more elaborate American variant of the European shepherd's hut. They were used, for example, to watch over the five million or so sheep in Wyoming at the start of the twentieth century. Reputedly invented by blacksmith James Candlish in 1884, the sheep herder's wagon was a remarkably efficient design with a transverse bed, table, benches, stove and washbasin. Although it used the bow-shaped canvas roof of the covered wagon, it was far more practical to live and sleep in. These compact wagons acted as the inspiration for a number of twentieth century American travel trailer designers. Restored or recreated versions are still in use today.

The Lure of Nature

In the second half of the nineteenth century, American health seekers and hunters, drawn to the interior by plentiful supplies of clean air and wildlife, felt increasingly confident in travelling west. Although localized conflicts with native Americans continued, most native tribes had been hounded close to extinction and were no longer seen as a threat. After the American Civil War, health seekers and hunters were joined by established settlers on trips into the wilderness as they turned their attention towards more peaceful pursuits.

One of these new pursuits was tourism. For a new and rapidly growing cohort of middle-class Americans along with some wealthy and adventurous European visitors, the great American landscapes became the sightseeing equivalent of Europe's castles and cathedrals. Prompted by the writings of nature-lovers and environmentalists such as John Muir, American city dwellers were reminded of the beauty that existed beyond the eastern seaboard. Muir emphasized the need to treat wilderness areas as places to be admired and protected rather than just exploited for their resources. Foresighted leaders such as President Ulysses S. Grant ensured that a number of America's wild places were preserved as national parks, with Yellowstone becoming the world's first national park in 1872. President Theodore Roosevelt would later create an additional five new parks and eighteen national monuments between 1901 and 1909.

When the Transcontinental Railroad was completed in 1869, tourists were given a new way to explore their natural surroundings in relative safety and comfort. Railroads, hotels and resorts built in and around the country's natural wonders lured wealthier tourists with train, hotel and sightseeing packages. In the late nineteenth century some of the wealthiest hired Pullman Palace Cars, luxurious self-contained railway carriages attached to regular train services and left at a tourist destination as a private hotel on wheels. For everyone else, and in particular the increasing number of independent-minded American tourists who found the formality and strict timetables of resort hotels and railroads stifling, there was an alternative – camping.

Murray's Rush

In 1869, church minister William H.H. Murray wrote a book called *Adventures in the Wilderness; or Camp-Life in the Adirondacks*. It was the first true camping guide to be published in America, encouraging health seekers, hunters and tourists to experience the health-giving qualities, sport and beauty of the region. They did so in droves. According to the Smithsonian Institution, 'within months of the book's release, the sleepy Adirondack region was transformed, as an unprecedented horde of 2,000 to 3,000 recreational campers, hunters and anglers arrived from New York, Boston, Hartford, Philadelphia and other cities'. This stampede came to be known as 'Murray's Rush', and at its peak the guidebook sold 500 copies a week. Other guidebooks followed in the late 1800s and early 1900s covering all aspects of camping, woodcraft and self-sufficiency.

The McMaster Camping Car

In the early 1890s the earliest-known American, purpose-built, horse-drawn RV appeared, albeit briefly, in Yellowstone, the world's first national park. It was also one of the first ever RVs available for public hire. Developed by Alonzo J. McMaster of Lockport, New York and patented in 1889, the McMaster Camping Car was a dedicated leisure camping vehicle. According to an 1892 brochure, 'the car can be owned by one or more families, or by clubs of young men, and provide a cheap, pleasant way to secure recreation and comfort in camping out.'

The McMaster Camping Car (USA, c1892)

In the mid-1880s McMaster had owned a fleet of horse-drawn omnibuses in Lockport called Herdic carriages, named after their inventor Peter Herdic from Pennsylvania. Similar to the ambulance wagon, these were lightweight vehicles with low floors and rear entrances. Bench seating was added for passengers along their sides. McMaster appears to have adapted a number of elements of Herdic's design into his radical new camping car. McMaster developed at least two versions of this novel vehicle that we know of, one weighing 1,400 pounds and a more elaborate version weighing 1,700 pounds. Either was therefore light enough to be drawn by two horses. The heavier camping car contained red plush bench seating along each side convertible into four beds, a fifth hammock underneath the car for the driver, a toilet room which was, according to the brochure, 'as large as on a Pullman sleeping car', two water tanks, wash bowl, a wardrobe with a removable door for use as a table and an ice chest. Two oil stoves were secured under the driver's seat and a curtain could be pulled around the front of the car 'to furnish entire seclusion for cooking operations'.

In 1889 McMaster went camping in his first camping car called *Niagara* and, based on positive feedback from admirers, decided to go into limited production under the name of McMaster Manufacturing Co., Lockport. He advertised the vehicle for sale locally and in 1890 he sold a second camping car called *Marion* to George L. Mason from Marion, Illinois for $1,200. Later that year McMaster exhibited a camping car at the Minneapolis Industrial Exposition, reputedly to much acclaim.

In May 1892, William Wallace Wylie and his partner Sam M. Wilson, who operated a moveable tent-camp touring company in Yellowstone National Park, purchased two of the camping cars. Since the mid-1880s, Wylie's camping operation had provided an economic alternative to the high-priced hotel tour of the park as well as offering an educational excursion of Yellowstone's spectacular landscape. With the addition of the McMaster Camping Cars, Wylie & Wilson could offer a somewhat exclusive twelve-day escorted tour in a comfortable, self-contained vehicle for groups of four with a driver for a mere $5 per day per person. One of the perks of this private tour was the opportunity to enjoy some secluded trout fishing at prime spots in the park. But according to Yellowstone historian Elizabeth Watry, the upstart McMaster Camping Car was viewed with hostility by the hotel and transportation companies, who were allied with the Northern Pacific Railroad cartel and were opposed to any competition. They tried to force Wylie & Wilson's new camping cars out of business through a range of means including spurious complaints about frightening the established operators' stagecoach horses and even going so far as to call for Wylie's arrest.

According to available evidence, the McMaster Camping Cars were only used within the park for the 1892 season. Wylie said much later in his autobiography 'I did not quit the use of these cars because of this attempt to put them out of use, but because they did not accommodate enough guests to make them practicable'. But the underhand tactics of established concession holders would not have helped Wylie & Wilson to win, let alone keep, new customers. Clearly, the McMaster Camping Car undermined the more conventional tourism schemes of the special interest groups of the period, and like many such ideas ahead of their time, was obstructed by those in favour of the status quo from obtaining the necessary momentum for success. It is still fitting though, that the world's first national park was home to what is probably America's first ever purpose-built RV. As for McMaster, his camping car venture was not as successful as hoped, since by 1895 he was forced to sell real estate to pay off bank debts. He later became the Health Inspector for Lockport from 1903 until 1910 and died in 1913.

Early 'Houses on Wheels'

Those who wanted to camp but avoid the stampedes of Murray's Rush developed their own methods of independent travel. Reports of horse-drawn wagons passing through US towns on leisure or health trips began to appear more widely in the 1870s. These vehicles were simply called 'houses on wheels' by reporters of the day. By the 1890s, newspaper accounts had begun to emerge in the USA of the exploits of the UK's gentlemen gypsies including Dr Gordon Stables and the Duke of Newcastle. These accounts may have encouraged more houses to be put on wheels in America.

For example, in 1892, we learn that M.E. Rose of Chadron, Nebraska 'has constructed an 8[ft] x 16[ft] house on wheels with all conveniences, in which to take his family camping'. A year later, Dick Stone makes a two-month journey from Fresno, California to Chicago to visit the World Fair in a house on wheels. That same year, the Dwinell family of Marshfield, Vermont, spent a week camping in their house on wheels at Malletts Bay.

In the mid to late 1890s we begin to see sketches of houses on wheels appear in regional US newspapers as well as more extensive descriptions of their owners and their journeys. Perhaps the most remarkable RV trip undertaken prior to 1900 was that of upholsterer Morgan Lasley and his family.

THE HOUSE ON WHEELS.

A JOLLY JAUNT FOR THE FAMILY

Above left: This was probably the first of several 'houses on wheels' built by Morgan Lasley between 1894 and 1905. Alternatively, it may have been his second wagon sketched prior to substantial modification (USA, 1897)

Above right: An unnamed builder from Kansas constructed for his invalid wife a 'summer house on wheels' in 1896 to visit the Rocky Mountains each year. As with Morgan Lasley, the idea came about as a result of the family physician suggesting that fresh air was the best cure for the builder's wife. The vehicle was simply built and lightweight. It invariably received the attention of 'kodakers' (photographers) during their summer trips (USA, 1896)

Above: Jonathan Olson from Altoona, Pennsylvania decided to travel around the world for pleasure in 1897 in a luxuriously-built three-roomed wagon with separate kitchen, bedroom, store room and a sliding door on one side. It is not known if he completed or even started his ambitious journey (USA, 1897)

Right: Church organist William Horatio Clarke from Reading, Massachusetts decided to undertake in 1899 a 'queer outing' to surrounding districts. For this outing he built for himself a simple 12ft by 8ft single-roomed wagon. Reference to his failing health is made in a report of his trip, suggesting once again the trip was made for health reasons (USA, 1899)

The Lasley Family

'I have lost hope for your wife; poor woman, she is going to die unless you go out camping with her.'

With these words from a foresighted family physician to Morgan Lasley about his wife Mary, the Lasley family set off in 1894 in their 'traveling palace' from Port Angeles in Washington. What was originally intended as a short trip to San Francisco for health reasons turned into a remarkable 6,666-mile, four-year journey across America to New York, ending in 1898. It was fully documented by the fascinated press of the day as well as in two books written by the family. Their wagon was certainly not, as Lasley claimed, the 'only house on wheels' at the time, but it was one of the first trans-American journeys made by choice rather than necessity in a vehicle of this kind.

Mr and Mrs Lasley were two of the most resourceful people imaginable. The Lasleys took their young children with them and had one more along the way. A dog kept guard. The idea to build the wagon belonged to Mrs Lasley, who also designed the interior and fittings. Lasley built the wagon to his wife's specifications, modifying it as they travelled and constructing a rudimentary cyclometer from an alarm clock to monitor mileage. According to reporters the interior was always kept neat and tidy.

Lasley found work wherever he could along the trail to pay for food and expenses. He sold photos and leaflets documenting their travels and even earned money as a fortune-teller. They attracted crowds wherever they went. But appalling roads, bad

The Lasley family and their 'house on wheels' (USA, 1898)

weather, starvation and thirst were never far away, and the trip required more than two dozen horses to complete. The account of their trip describes the vast range of treatment they received at the hands of fellow travellers and locals, from the hospitable to the hostile. The dangers of rural travel at the time are vividly described. A typical entry from Lasley's account of the trip reads:

'Nothing special occurred (barring night attack of wolves and mosquitos, camping out among bandits, crossing dangerous rivers, surrounded by deadly reptiles, breaking of the wagon tongue in dangerous place, the wheels breaking down, being misguided, etc.) until we arrived at Wagoner, I.T., Oct 3rd.'

For contemporary RV owners who think that they have just returned from a difficult trip, a reading of Lasley's *Across America in the Only House on Wheels* of 1898 may offer a useful sense of perspective. The Lasley family found the overall experience positive, however, describing the trip as 'showing how a poor but ambitious family can turn disaster into benefit, and be healthy, have a good living, enjoy life, see all and be happy'.

Camp Cars, Touring Limousines and Buses (1900-1915)

When the automobile arrived in America at the turn of the century, it was soon clear that the new invention would have a major impact on tourism. Automobiles covered the country's long distances quicker than trains and, thanks to Henry Ford, became affordable faster than anywhere else in the world. Most significantly, they offered personal freedom to travel at will.

Although there are some reports of unmodified automobiles and trucks being used for camping holidays in the early 1900s, the first type of American motorized vehicle to be adapted for recreation appears to be the 'camp car' in about 1904. These were goods trucks converted for sleeping and were used mainly by hunters. They were generally self-built, cumbersome and could not travel easily to remote areas without getting stuck on the poor roads of the day.

According to *The Automobile* of 12 October 1905, Roy Faye and Freeman Young set off with two others from Cambridge, Massachusetts to Maine in 1905 in their self-built camp car for a few weeks of hunting. Their vehicle was a more powerful model of a Rambler camp car they had built in 1904 about which little is known. The 1905 version was built on a 40hp Thomas Flyer chassis, had folding beds, ice chest, electric, gas

A Rambler Camp Car (USA, 1904)

and oil lamps and a 'place for Mr Faye's bird dogs'. It had a unique accessory – a tall, wireless communications mast that could be erected in minutes at camp for keeping in touch with the outside world.

On 8 November 1906, *The Automobile* reported on another camp car owned by Faye, calling it the Matheson Hunting Car. In connection with Faye's appointment as New England distributor for The Matheson Company of New York, the newspaper describes Faye's camp car as a 40hp Matheson 'which he has transformed into a hunting and camping machine of very novel type'. Matheson vehicles were known for their strong engines and hill-climbing ability. It included four bunks,

a painted black canvas roof, a hot water system that used the engine's radiator, electric lighting and an ice box under the chassis.

It seems then that Faye had owned three camp cars – a 1904 Rambler, a 1905 Thomas Flyer and a 1906 Matheson. These were some of the earliest examples of camp cars in America, perhaps crudely built but a step up in comfort levels from tent camping. The camp car would not be seen in numbers, however until the new Ford Model TT truck appeared onto the automobile scene in 1917. The Ford was both affordable and adaptable, and led to many self-built camp cars being built using a Ford chassis over the next twenty years.

A Welch Touring Limousine (USA, 1909)

As engines increased in power, chassis could be lengthened and weight increased. This led to the development of long-distance touring automobiles called touring limousines, first conceived in France by de Dietrich in 1904 (see pages 78-79). They were intended for use by wealthy travellers and offered far greater luxury than the camp car. In 1909, The Welch Motor Car Company of America produced a specially lengthened 80hp six-cylinder vehicle for actor Nat Goodwin to be used for touring purposes. It seated up to eight people and its rear seat could be converted to a transverse bed suspended on straps. It also included bath, refrigerator, crockery and numerous small cupboards and lockers. It weighed 3 tons and was said to 'get over the ground splendidly'.

Pierce-Arrow followed Welch a year later with the Pierce-Arrow Touring Landau. The company's first landau was constructed for Pierce-Arrow president George Birge and shown at the 1910 Madison Avenue Motor Show in New York, arousing much interest. It had a 66hp engine and cost $8,250, a small fortune at the time. It included considerable luggage space on the roof and at the rear for long term touring, automatic folding steps and a sink supplied by a water tank under the chassis. Although the rear seat and back cushion could be arranged to form a bed, owners were generally expected to be able to afford hotel accommodation. The interior was made of tooled leather and a telephone could be installed for communication between the owner and chauffeur. It is thought that the vehicle was built only to order for a very small number of fortunate customers.

Another luxury limousine that explored the camping possibilities of the automobile appeared in 1911. In 1908, Thomas Coleman du Pont, a member of the Delaware-based family that founded the DuPont conglomerate, decided to build

A Pierce-Arrow Touring Landau (USA, 1910)

Above: The Dupont Camping Auto (USA, c1911)

Below: The Dupont Camping Auto with balloon silk awnings (USA, c1911)

and finance a highway in Delaware to help the state's economy and increase tourism. Construction got underway in about 1911. As an engineer, he wanted to oversee the construction of the road, and, in the absence of any alternative accommodation in the area, du Pont commissioned a 'camping auto'.

Built on a 45hp Stoddard-Dayton chassis, the vehicle was tailor-made for the job at hand. It contained modular elongated lockers along its sides to hold maps and construction drawings as well as boxes for two tents, a 6-foot mattress, gas stove, ice box, battery and camping chairs. The camping car's most unusual features were its two attachable tents, made out of waterproof balloon silk instead of canvas. When fully assembled, the camping auto provided three rooms with the bedroom as part of the vehicle in the central section. The Du Pont Highway (now US 13 and 113) was finally opened in 1924 at a cost of $4 million.

Luxury tourers such as those developed by Welch, Pierce-Arrow and Du Pont were something of an evolutionary dead-end in RV terms. They were too expensive for the vast majority. Their main purpose was to serve as comfortable private transport between hotels, so sleeping facilities were rudimentary or non-existent. The Ford Model T and its goods-carrying cousin, the TT, would soon come to offer consumers far greater camping customization options at much lower prices.

A Vacation in a Bus

A unique RV appeared on American roads in 1915 – a double-decker bus. The travels of its owners, the Conklin family, were widely reported in the US media of that year. Roland P. Conklin was the proprietor of two bus companies in New York and Chicago. Described in August 1915 by *The New York Times* as 'a flat on tires', Conklin's 'gypsy van' transported his family and staff on a transcontinental trip from New York to San Francisco. It was a 25ft-long converted bus with a 65hp motor, bunk beds for six people, a shower-bath, folding lavatory, multiple ingeniously-built cupboards, icebox, galley, gas generator and batteries, electric lights and a roof garden. The steps to the upper level could be folded to create a tea or card table. The family had the foresight to bring along a motor bike 'tender' to scout out the road ahead, just as the valet of Dr Gordon Stables had done on a tricycle in Britain in 1885. The Conklin family were supported by a three-man crew for driving, cooking and other duties.

The bus had to be rescued from a ditch by the local fire brigade on the first day of the trip, but there were no further reports of trouble. Conklin helped to publicize the poor condition of roads at the time by complaining bitterly about them to the press in his trip updates. With an estimated weight of between 7 and 8 tons, the journey must have been slow-going and the fuel bills large. The Smithsonian Institution comments, 'The family's journey was so widely publicized that their invention became the general template for generations of motorhomes'. Whilst a converted double-decker bus would rarely be seen again in the US RV world, the trip would certainly have inspired many to take to the road in their own 'gypsy van'.

The Conklin Family Auto Bus (USA, 1915)

The interior of the Conklin Auto Bus (USA, 1915)

Auto Camping (1905-1930)

By far the most popular form of motorized recreation in America at the start of the twentieth century was 'auto camping' – filling an automobile with camping gear and heading into the wilds. The invention of the automobile allowed Americans to take their instinctive love of the outdoors to a new level. Unlike the UK, where early RVs were predominantly solid-walled, fixed-roof caravans designed to insulate their occupants from the extremes of British weather, the first mass-produced RVs in the USA were diverse combinations of lightweight automobiles, trailers and tents. The growing number of national parks was made more accessible by newly-built roads, giving everyone who could afford an automobile the chance to visit these remote areas. The arrival of the low-cost Ford Model T in 1908 led to an auto camping free-for-all that would later stretch the country's national parks and roads to the limit.

There were three overlapping phases in the phenomenal growth of auto camping between 1905 and 1930: camping with a standard automobile; camping with a tent trailer; and finally camping with specialized camping vehicles.

An autocamper at Yellowstone National Park (USA, c1915)

First came camping with automobiles. In order to keep costs down and demand high for this new pastime, automobile manufacturers made minimal changes to production automobiles. Specialist auto camping accessory companies sprang up out of nowhere, offering a wide range of auto camping accessories such as seats that could be turned into beds, canvas that could be tied to an automobile to form an awning, mattresses that could be rolled up and strapped onto running boards and camping equipment such as ice boxes and stoves that could fit onto the sides or rear of an auto. Owner modifications of automobiles to accommodate these accessories were common.

Second, in the mid-1910s, came the tent trailer. Starting out as simple box trailers attached to automobiles for carrying luggage, tent trailers emerged as a solution to the problem of where to store increasing volumes of camping gear that was leaving little room left in the automobile for passengers. Not only were tent trailers a more efficient way of storing camping equipment, they also allowed the tow vehicle to be used separately for exploration or daily use when not camping.

Over time, the tent became an integral part of the trailer. Instead of removing the tent and setting it up elsewhere, the tent was fixed to the trailer and unfolded when needed. The trailer body was used as a base for sleeping and for storage. These were known as 'pop-up trailers' and were small, light and easily towed by less-powerful automobiles.

Tent trailer historian Joel Silvey's extensive research indicates that the oldest known pop-up trailer built for the specific purpose of camping was made by the Detroit Trailer Company in 1913. The Los Angeles Trailer Company, Campbell Folding Trailer Company, Auto-Kamp Equipment Company and several others soon followed. Silvey notes that by the time of the USA's entry into the First World War in 1917, at least twenty tent trailer manufacturers were operating. Most pre-1920 tent trailer manufacturers were concentrated in the Detroit area to take advantage of proximity to the major automobile manufacturers of the period.

Although the First World War slowed the tent trailer industry, growth resumed again strongly after 1920. During the 1920s tent trailers became larger and more elaborate, incorporating doors, windows and mattresses or folding beds. Their affordability and light weight, combined with the completion of new roads to wilderness areas and vacation destinations in the south, led to a significant increase in the popularity of auto camping nationwide.

The Auto Kamp Equipment Company were one of the best-known tent trailer manufacturers. Based in the Great

A self-built 'picnic tender' carrying a table, gas stove and food (USA, 1909)

The Campbell Folding Camping Trailer (USA, 1914)

Lakes Region, they developed a simple trailer suited to mass production and was accordingly very affordable. Having begun production in 1916, by the end of the 1920s they were producing a range of tent trailers including a large 'bungalow' at the top end of their price range.

The Warner Prairie Schooner Camping Trailer (USA, 1916)

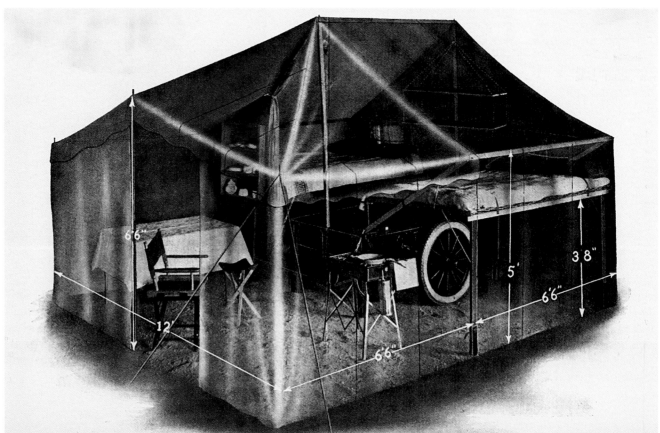

The Auto-Kamp Bungalow Model No. 5 (USA, 1929)

Camping Autos (1915-25)

The third RV movement of this period was a specialized camping vehicle called the 'camping auto'. Coachbuilders or camping outfitters would take a standard auto body and convert it into sleeping quarters in often ingenious ways. By incorporating beds and a range of other camping equipment into the body, the need for a trailer was eliminated. The camping auto was perhaps the most sophisticated camping option available during the 1920s, but it was more expensive and less flexible than the tent trailer. Consequently, it sold in far smaller numbers.

Gustav de Bretteville of San Francisco was one of the earliest camping auto makers. In 1915 he developed a 'telescopic camping apartment' to be attached to the rear of a vehicle chassis. An enclosed box telescoped out to the rear and rested on legs in an early version of today's RV slide-out compartment. Whilst the term 'apartment' in the name is perhaps optimistic, de Bretteville managed to cram into the space a double bed, electric lighting, gas stove, table, an exhaust-run water heater, drawers and storage areas. Apparently, it could be added to or removed from the vehicle in fifteen minutes by an amateur.

The Lamsteed Kampkar was a larger and more elaborate camping auto than de Bretteville's. It was designed by Samuel B. Lambert, a member of the family who owned Lambert Pharmacal Co., the makers of the mouthwash Listerine. As Prohibition came into force in the USA in 1920, brewer

Gustav de Bretteville's Automobile Telescope Touring Apartment (USA, 1916)

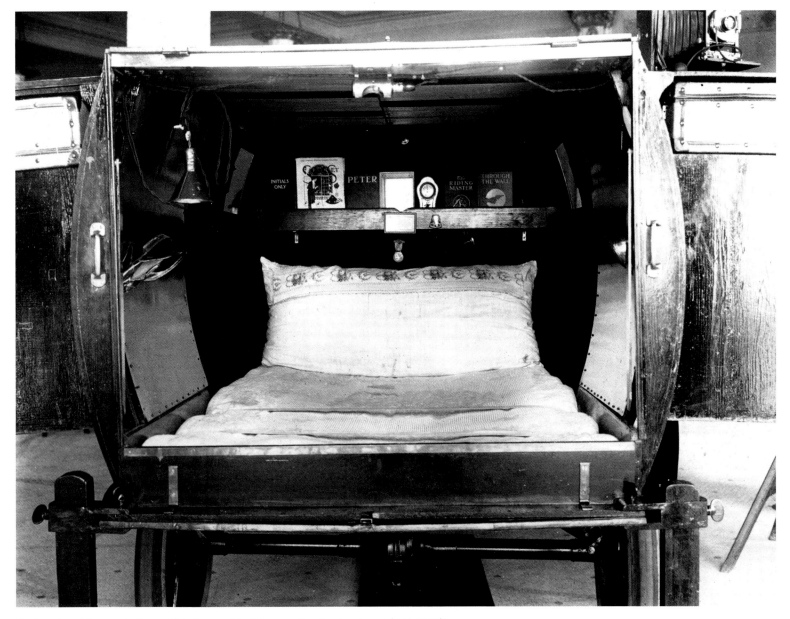

The interior of Gustav de Bretteville's Automobile Telescope Touring Apartment (USA, 1916)

Anheuser-Busch (of Budweiser fame) was forced to diversify into new businesses. One of their more unusual new product lines was vehicle production, a spin-off from their beverage delivery vehicle division. The company assumed manufacturing of the Kampkar from around 1921 for about a decade.

The Lamsteed Kampkar came in kit form, allowing a Ford Model T and other vehicles to be converted into a camping vehicle in a claimed six hours for a price of $535.

The kit created a vehicle that included two side-folding beds enclosed in tents, folding table, stove, lockers and a range of camping equipment. Although more expensive than simple autocampers, the Lamsteed remained a practical, mid-priced RV option for some.

In 1921 Frank Zagelmeyer of Bay City, Michigan created the Zagelmeyer Auto Camp Company, building a number of simple camp trailers. He was best known however for his Kamper Kar,

first advertised in 1925 and described as 'a completely equipped, self-contained, rigid frame, canvas-covered camping body'. Its party piece was a roof that lifted at the same time as the side beds were lowered. Zagelmeyer also made a Pullman coach in the late 1920s and received a patent for a new type of locking tow ball hitch. The Zagelmeyer Kamper Kar was perhaps the most elaborate of the camping autos, but they were to represent the last of a line of hybrid RVs from the 1920s with increasingly apparent disadvantages. They were not cheap, mechanically complex and inflexible when used as everyday transport at home.

Overall, the 1920s was a decade of experimentation and trend-setting in affordable camping vehicles, allowing millions to enjoy the RV hobby for the first time. Wide-ranging permutations of the autocamper were explored, improved upon or discarded, whilst patent-filing of the latest design to prevent copycats was rife. The tent trailer and camping auto co-existed with the 'housecar', or motorhome, throughout this period, meeting different needs and price points until all were eclipsed by the arrival of a new kid on the block, the travel trailer, from about 1930.

Above: Dr A.A. Foster and family from Dallas, Texas, on vacation in Washington, D.C. in a Lamsteed Kampkar (USA, c1920)

Below: The Zagelmeyer Kamper Kar (USA, 1925)

Promoting Nature Tourism – The Four Vagabonds (1915-24)

'It often seemed to me that we were a luxuriously equipped expedition going forth to seek discomfort.'

from *Under the Maples* by
John Burroughs, 1921

In 1915, the idea of using automobiles to explore nature received a strong boost from a most unlikely source – a small group of the country's political, environmental and industrial leaders. They became known as the Four

Vagabonds. They were Henry Ford of the Ford Motor Company, Thomas Edison, inventor, Harvey Firestone, founder of the Firestone Tire and Rubber Company and naturalist John Burroughs (who passed away in 1921). Between 1915 and 1924 they went on a series of summer camping trips. The publicity surrounding the trips captured the public's imagination, stirred an appetite for travel into the wild places of America and helped to stimulate a camping and RV boom.

Henry Ford, Thomas Edison, President Warren Harding and Harvey Firestone at Firestone Camp. John Burroughs had passed away earlier that year (USA, 1921)

The idea of a group camping trip was hatched when Ford and Burroughs visited Edison in Florida in 1914. Their first trip was as a trio in 1916 to the New England Adirondacks and Green Mountains, the location of Murray's Rush (see page 106). Ford was unable to join them that year, but between 1918 and 1924 the group, along with selected guests (including President Warren Harding in 1921 and President Coolidge in 1924), visited the mountains of West Virginia as well as Tennessee, North Carolina, Virginia, New England and Michigan.

A large number of passenger cars and vans (over fifty in 1919) accompanied the trips to take the travellers, staff, film crew, photographer, camping and cooking equipment. Their tents were individually monogrammed and lit by Edison's lights and generator. On later trips a circular, lazy Susan-style table seating twenty people was used with waiters in attendance. These excursions were widely reported in American newspapers. They continued after Burroughs' death in 1921, but by 1924 the trips were gathering so much attention that it was decided to stop them. Photographic records of the trip along with a number of the motor vehicles involved are part of the collection of the Henry Ford Museum of American Innovation in Dearborn, Michigan.

There is no doubt that the Four Vagabonds undertook these trips in part to promote their own products and ideas. But their greatest contribution to recreation in America was their foresightedness in promoting automobiles, tents and the American wilderness as a complete and irresistible package to American consumers. If this group and their eminent guests survived camping in the wilds, even for just a few days and with no shortage of creature comforts, anyone could.

A postcard of the Paradise Valley Camp Ground in Mount Rainier National Park. Created in 1899, Mount Rainier was the first US national park to permit automobiles. Autocamping in the park increased significantly following the camping trips of The Four Vagabonds (USA, 1925)

Getting Together – The Tin Can Tourists (1919)

America's early RV users began to get organized in 1919. The 'Tin Can Tourists' was America's first RV club. They formed at Desoto Park in Tampa, Florida in 1919 in order to 'unite fraternally all autocampers'. A secondary objective was to clearly distinguish those who camped by choice from those who travelled due to economic hardship. The confusion between the two groups caused much frustration to early recreational campers.

According to current Tin Can Tourist 'Royal Chief' Terry Bone, the group was named after the Ford Model T used by many members and known affectionately as the Tin Lizzie. Members' vehicles would be recognized by a tin can on their automobile radiators which qualified them for discounted fuel at selected gas stations. Joining the group required learning a secret handshake, password and the organisation's song. The head of

the organisation was called the 'Royal Can Opener' which was changed to 'Royal Chief' in 1935. Meetings of 'Canners', known as Homecomings, Winter Conventions or Going Home meets, were held around the country, with the Winter Convention taking place in Florida each year. By 1921, the organisation had 17,000 members in the USA and Canada which swelled to over 100,000 in 1924. Initially regarded with some scepticism by local communities and the media, the Tin Can Tourists were by the 1930s broadly welcomed. During the 1930s, trailer manufacturers would often attend the Canners' camps in order to sell their trailers.

The major contribution of Tin Can Tourists to RV history in America was the creation of a community of like-minded people who could come together regardless of the type of RV they owned. They cemented the RV as a recognized, democratic and enjoyable leisure pursuit, creating in the process an important social and photographic record of camping with vehicles during the 1920s and 1930s. The organisation continued to hold meets into the 1980s and was re-formed in 1998.

The Tin Can Tourist Convention at Arcadia, Florida (USA, 1931)

US Housecars of the 1920s

Whilst 'autocampers' in the 1920s mostly used cost-effective tent trailers to get out into the wild, the 'housecar' or motorhome offered a more luxurious if costlier option. Buyers could choose between purpose-built housecars offered by a small number of manufacturers or build their own. Self-builders usually converted a truck or bus with highly variable results. The housecar, which was more at home on purpose-built roads than tracks in the wilderness, became more popular as roads slowly improved during the 1920s. For example, the Dixie Highway from northern states to Miami was built between 1915 and 1929, opening up the south to housecar-owning northerners.

The Wiedman Company offered an interesting compromise between purpose- and self-built housecars by making 'camp bodies' that were factory installed or shipped to customers for mounting on a chassis of their choice. Other automobile or truck

Above: Mr. W.A. Harris and family from Texas visiting Washington, D.C. Their housecar was reputedly made from beaverboard, a material made of highly compressed wood pulp (USA, 1924)

Below: A Pierce-Arrow housecar (USA, 1926)

Above: Mr. W.M. O'Donnell and family from Detroit and their 'bungalow auto' in Washington, D.C. (USA, 1926)

Below: The *Burn Ballad Bungalow* of June and Farrar Burn and family in Washington, D.C. June was a writer and Farrar a singer and songwriter who performed at campgrounds during their travels (USA, 1929)

manufacturers experimented in a limited way with housecars including REO, Hudson Essex, Graham Brothers and Pierce-Arrow, but there were inadequate numbers of wealthy and adventurous clients to justify going into serious production. During the 1920s housecar manufacturers were still grappling with the noise, comfort and vibration issues associated with placing a wooden frame on a truck chassis designed to carry goods. Wealthy customers generally had little tolerance for such shortcomings. Nevertheless, the housecar remained a niche RV product for long-distance travellers throughout the 20s and 30s, playing a supporting role alongside the RV design that would come to dominate the 1930s around the world – the travel trailer.

The Travel Trailer

During the 1920s, as the American road network expanded and automobiles continued to become more powerful, a new RV design started to become viable – the 'house trailer'. The house trailer was the American equivalent of the British caravan and over time became known as the travel trailer. These solid-walled trailers towed by an automobile had been seen in the 1910s – the RV/MH Hall of Fame's Earl Trailer of 1913 is perhaps the earliest known example – but were generally too heavy by comparison with tent trailers to be towed by early, low-powered automobiles. By the 1920s the caravan was becoming the RV of choice in Britain because of its flexibility. Caravan owners could keep their existing vehicles for towing, leave the caravan parked on arrival and go exploring in the tow vehicle. US travel trailers would gradually gain favour for the same reasons. Tent trailers were the most popular form of trailer, but uncommitted consumers wanted more comfort. The travel trailer was the answer and would mobilize Americans in their millions.

Unburdened by the caravan-building traditions of their British cousins, American travel trailer designers of the 1920s and '30s were free to come up with bigger and bolder ideas better suited to American conditions. They did not disappoint. Just as in Britain and France, some of the most radical American travel trailer ideas came from the aviation industry. American leadership in aviation manufacturing during the 1920s had an important side-effect: a good understanding of lightweight, streamlined construction techniques. It was no surprise then that some of the pioneers of American travel trailer design of the 1920s and '30s came from the aviation industry. Two of them, Glenn Curtiss and Hawley Bowlus, used aviation construction techniques and materials that had a lasting influence on RV design worldwide. Another pioneer, Wally Byam, was not from the aviation industry but used its forms and materials to create perhaps the world's most recognisable RV – the Airstream.

Glenn H. Curtiss and The Aerocar

'Glenn, it's a darned shame we have to leave the women-folks at home every time we hark to the call of the wild. Can't we figure out some scheme to make them comfortable, and enable them to enjoy the gypsy life as much as we do?'

George Carl Adams to his half-brother
Glenn Curtiss (c1918)

Glenn H. Curtiss was an inventor, engineer, designer, pilot, racing driver, developer and philanthropist. Amongst his many achievements was earning the title of 'Fastest Man in The World' between 1904 and 1911 thanks to his self-built motorcycles, one of which in 1907 reached a speed of 136.36mph. In 1908, Curtiss designed and flew an aircraft called the June Bug a distance of 5,080ft, in the process making the first pre-announced heavier-than-air flight and winning the Scientific American Trophy. In 1911, Curtiss flew the world's first seaplane and successfully launched a plane from a ship.

Curtiss came relatively late to the RV world – he didn't start designing and building trailers for leisure purposes until he was in his forties. As a keen camper and hunter, he and his half-brother George C. Adams decided in about 1918 to seek a way to bring their wives and families along on their trips in greater comfort. This homespun inspiration led to two major RV initiatives, the Adams Motorbungalo in 1918 followed by the iconic Curtiss Aerocar a decade later. Both were designed using techniques and materials borrowed from the aircraft industry. Their good looks, light weight and safety features made them some of the most desirable RVs of the period.

A photo of Curtiss' aircraft workshop at Long Island in about 1919 (overleaf) is a poignant illustration of the close relationship between Curtiss' planes and trailers. The simple utility trailer carrying an aircraft engine gives little indication of the sophisticated leisure trailers to come, but the image demonstrates the wealth of aviation design and engineering expertise at Curtiss' command as he built some of the most advanced recreational vehicles ever seen.

During the First World War, thanks to his aircraft building prowess, Curtiss had been commissioned by the US Army's aviation section to build a range of training aircraft (the 'Jenny') as well as seaplanes. The pressure of delivering these aircraft as well as managing two factories and over 20,000 workers was intense. Curtiss needed a diversion.

Curtiss would often visit the remote areas of New York State and Florida on hunting and fishing trips together with his half-brother Adams. In 1917 Adams had formed a company in Long Island making utility trailers called the Adams Trailer Corporation.

Above: Glenn Curtiss and his V8 motorcycle (USA, 1907)

Below: Glenn Curtiss and plane (USA, c1911)

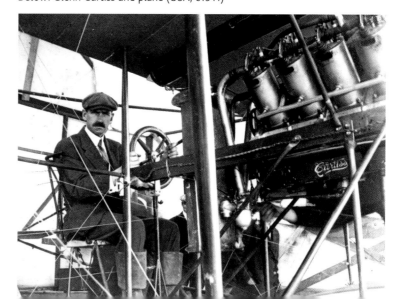

At Adams' request, in about 1918 Curtiss designed a prototype for a new type of camping trailer. It went into production in 1919 at both the Adams trailer factory and the Curtiss aircraft factory. Called the Adams Motorbungalo, the trailer had a hard top, fold-out beds, kitchenette and electric lighting. Most importantly it weighed only 900 pounds, allowing it to be towed, using a conventional ball and socket joint, by a wide range of vehicles.

Curtiss and Adams went on to design and build a number of Motorbungalo models. The 1921 and 1922 Motorbungalo brochures list four variants based on two main designs – the Model M Closed Motorbungalo De Lux and the Model R Closed Folding Motorbungalo. A Model S was the same as the Model R with modifications, whilst a Model T was the same as the Model S but with a kitchenette and wardrobe. An extensive range of camping equipment was made available for sale to accompany the trailer.

Despite increasing the number of models and receiving a patent for his design, Curtiss found sales were challenging

A utility trailer at Curtiss' Long Island plant (USA, c1919)

The Adams Motorbungalo (USA, 1920)

Above: A group of Adams Motorbungalos at camp. Two deluxe versions (left and right) and (centre) a standard version (USA, 1920)

Left: The Aero Coupler fifth wheel designed by Glenn Curtiss. It consisted of a pneumatic aircraft wheel within a square frame placed horizontally over the rear axle of the tow vehicle to receive the trailer's hitch (USA, c1930)

during the post-war recession. As hybrid camping trailers, Motorbungalos were perhaps too luxurious and costly for Model T owners but not grand enough for the wealthy. The company was dissolved in 1924. The Motorbungalo nevertheless proved to be an early forerunner of the American travel trailer of the 1930s and the development springboard for Curtiss' next project – the Curtiss Aerocar.

Curtiss' Aerocar was conceived over several years between the demise of the Adams Trailer Corporation in 1924 and the launch of the Aerocar in 1928. Building on his wealth of knowledge gained in the aircraft construction industry and lessons learned from the Motorbungalo, Curtiss developed the Aerocar using lightweight plane construction methods. To these he added a unique 'fifth wheel' towing hitch, the Aero Coupler, which improved stability and thus safety at higher speeds. As well as designing beautiful vehicles, Curtiss' legacy in the RV world includes helping to make trailers safer.

Curtiss posing with an Aerocar built for M.D. Graves of Pittsfield, Mass. with Graves' Cadillac. The photo is taken in front of Curtiss' house in Miami Springs, Florida (USA, 1929)

The Aerocar frame followed aircraft design principles including braced cross-wires (USA, c1930)

The Aerocar suspension, reputed to make occupants feel they were floating on air (USA, c1930)

In 1928 an entrepreneur and friend of Curtiss, Carl G. Fisher, wrote of the Aerocar, 'Glenn Curtiss has produced the greatest trailer that was ever made in America'. Unlike the Motorbungalo, Aerocars did away with any camping pretences. They were unashamedly luxurious houses on wheels driven mainly by chauffeurs. Generally built to order for private clients, top end models such as Model 161-BPC cost $8,500. This model offered optional air conditioning and a raised viewing cockpit for occupants, who were permitted to ride in the trailer in transit. The cockpit incorporated a speedometer, compass, windscreen wipers and chauffeur intercom. Exact production number are unknown but estimates suggest up to 1,000 Aerocars were built between 1928 and 1940.

Despite Curtiss' untimely death in 1930, his Aerocars continued to be produced under licence at two factories in Michigan and Florida until 1940. With the Great Depression in full swing in 1930, the Aerocar found new uses. To travelling

sales representatives, it offered a cost-effective means of making a sale to distant or reluctant customers. It was soon adopted by a wide range of businesses as a mobile showroom or office. The Aerocar was also used as a school bus, ambulance, passenger transport vehicle and even a horse box. It was used extensively to transport passengers between airports, stations and luxury hotels. Some examples of commercial Aerocars are included in Chapter Eight.

Aerocars inspired other designers of the day, including industrial designer Brooks Stevens who in 1936 designed his Zephyr Land Cruiser based on a Curtiss Aerocar for photographer William Woods Plankinton Jr (see page 142). An equally luxurious model was made in 1938 for Dr Hubert Eaton named *The Vagabond*, now in the Petersen Automotive Museum in Los Angeles. The machines, achievements and legacies of Glenn Curtiss can be explored more fully at the Glenn H. Curtiss Museum in Hammondsport, New York.

The Bowlus Road Chief

William Hawley Bowlus was the creator of the first aluminium-riveted trailer in 1934. Like Curtiss, he applied his knowledge of flying machine design to the world of RVs. Bowlus flew his first glider at the age of ten. He designed, built and flew a number of small aircraft and gliders, breaking a number of glider flying records, but is best known in the aviation world for supervising the construction of Charles Lindbergh's aircraft *Spirit of St. Louis* in which Lindbergh crossed the Atlantic solo and non-stop in 1927. He trained many glider pilots and in 1931 formed a gliding school in New York with German glider and RV pioneer Wolf Hirth (see pages 157-159).

Bowlus built a number of lightweight canvas trailers to transport his gliders. He often had to camp at windy launch sites waiting for the right weather conditions. Seeking a more comfortable place to sleep than a tent which risked blowing away, Bowlus started exploring how he could convert his glider trailers into accommodation, much as Piggott Bros. had done with aircraft trailers in the UK after the First World War (see page 42). Although an early canvas prototype did not meet with his wife's approval, it was a forerunner of the monocoque style of trailer that Bowlus would become known for. He decided to move away from canvas and instead used 'Duralumin', an aluminium alloy that was as strong as steel but one third its weight. Developed in Germany and used by Junkers in the First World War, Duralumin was used in the manufacture of a range of aircraft and airships and was a familiar material to Bowlus. Its only negative was that Duralumin panels deteriorated if welded, so had to be riveted instead. Placed over a tubular steel frame, Duralumin was the key to both the light weight and stunning looks of Bowlus trailers.

Between 1934 and 1936 Bowlus produced dozens (estimates range between 80 and 200) of RVs at the Bowlus Teller factory (Teller was the company secretary). He reputedly produced four models – the Motor Chief, Road Chief, Papoose and Trail-Ur-Boat. The Papoose was the smallest trailer, measuring 11ft 6in long and weighing only 317kg. It was conceived primarily for use by travelling salesmen. The larger trailer, the Road Chief, was the most popular model. It was 18ft long but still weighed only 500kg. Bowlus' travel trailers had the unique feature of a front entry door, which despite giving the trailers a strong aerodynamic performance in wind tunnel tests, was not always practical in daily use. The Motor Chief was a motorized version of the Road Chief and built in very small numbers. It was a forerunner of the modern motorhome with flushing toilet, shower, hot and cold water and a refrigerator.

Bowlus trailers ranged in price from $750 for the Papoose to over $7,500 for the Motor Chief. With options on bigger models such as a cocktail bar, leather cushions and an intercom system between trailer and driver, they appealed in particular to the wealthy. As the Great Depression took hold, they became difficult to sell. When sales did not meet expectations, the company ran into difficulty paying its suppliers and the company went into receivership in 1936. But Bowlus' contributions to aeronautics and his transfer of aircraft construction techniques and materials into RVs of the 1930s are both lasting and invaluable. Well-preserved examples of original Bowlus trailers are some of the most expensive vintage RVs available today.

Gene Enos, equestrian director and announcer for the Russell Brothers Circus, with his Bowlus Road Chief in Bloomington, Illinois (USA, 1936)

Wally Byam and Airstream

'Adventure is where you find it, any place, every place, except at home in the rocking chair.'

Wally Byam

Airstream is today perhaps the most recognized RV brand in the world. The company is the only survivor from over 400 American trailer manufacturers operating before the Second World War. Its shining aluminium 'silver bullets' still turn heads wherever they go.

Airstream was formally created by Wally Byam in 1936, but Byam began building trailers of his own on a limited scale under the Airstream name from 1931. Starting his working life as a publisher, Byam also loved the outdoors. But his first wife Marion hated camping, so he decided to make something more comfortable. He created new designs for self-build travel trailers which were available by mail order for $5. They were so well received that customers asked if he would build them ready-made trailers. Byam agreed, providing kits,

shells and completed trailers from his Los Angeles workshop. His customers were given the opportunity to visit Byam's premises during construction and suggest improvements – customization was welcome. Despite the onset of the Great Depression, there were enough orders from travelling salesmen and others for Byam to leave publishing and go into the trailer-making business full time.

Byam went on to make a number of early Airstream trailer models including the 12ft Airlite, the 14ft Torpedo and Torpedo Junior, the 13.5ft Silver Cloud Junior and 16ft Silver Cloud. An 18ft Mobile Home was also produced for long-term occupation by 'circus people, carnival operators, oil workers and engineers'. The Airstream Torpedo Car Cruiser was teardrop-shaped, made of plywood and incorporated a lowered floor to increase internal headroom. Its shape would provide the template for all future Airstream models.

Byam's next trailer was to become an icon. He made his new trailer more liveable by moving the entrance to the side and incorporated the Torpedo's low floor between the axles. These changes required a modification of construction technique from monocoque to semi-monocoque. Most significantly the exterior of the trailer was made of Duralumin. The Airstream Clipper (see page 9) was born.

Named after the 'Pan Am Clipper' aeroplane, the Airstream Clipper also included a water pump, chemical toilet, ice box and gas stove. It was produced in limited quantities to the special order of each client. By producing them to order, Byam had no need to carry the financial burden of high inventories that had caused problems for Bowlus.

Byam continued to sell his non-aluminium models in parallel to the Clipper up to the start of the Second World War. At prices ranging from $550 to $1,000 they represented good value and were far more affordable than the Clipper, especially for families and travelling salesmen in the Depression era. By comparison, Clipper models ranged in price from $1,465 to $5,200.

In 1939 Byam produced a twin-axle version of the Clipper called the Superliner. It was to be the last new Airstream model before the onset of war. During the Second World War, aluminium was classified as a critical war material and not available for civilian use. The US War Production Board also ordered that all trailer manufacturing should cease unless approved for government use. So along with other trailer manufacturers, Airstream stopped production and Byam went to work for an aircraft company. The aircraft manufacturing experience Byam gained during this time was the catalyst for the next generation of post-war Airstreams when production resumed in 1947.

An Airstream Torpedo (USA, c1930s)

An Airstream Silver Bullet (USA, c1930s)

An Airstream Silver Cloud (USA, c1930s)

An Airstream Clipper Twin Axle (USA, c1930s)

The Travel Trailer Boom Years (1929-1937)

Travel trailers took a major leap forward in 1930s America. Ironically, the Great Depression of 1929-39 increased demand for trailers. Many unemployed workers travelled in trailers in search of jobs whilst others were evicted from their permanent homes or downsized to a movable home to save money. The tent trailers of the 1920s had satisfied the need for short-term camping in comfort, but they were not suited to extended family trips or long-term accommodation. The solid-walled trailer offered year-round protection from the weather.

During the 1930s, the self-built trailer became highly popular due to its low cost. They were built by individuals in their tens of thousands and were often made using plans sold by trailer manufacturers or published widely in magazines such as *Popular Mechanics*. As automobile production line manufacturing processes filtered through to trailer manufacturing, ready-made travel trailers became much more affordable, and became the largest selling RV product in the mid to late 1930s.

The Covered Wagon company was the first to make affordable travel trailers in large numbers. It was founded in 1929 by Arthur Sherman. Company legend has it that Sherman, a bacteriologist from Detroit, took a trailer tent on vacation in 1926. It took Sherman over half an hour to erect the tent in the rain despite assurances from the salesman that it could be done in ten minutes. So Sherman decided to build a tent trailer of his own. This he did together with a local cabinet maker – it was 9ft long, had a floor that could be lowered and was nicknamed by his children *The Covered Wagon* after the wagons of early American settlers. As is often the case in RV history, Sherman's prototype was seen by others who wanted their own and led Sherman into leaving his laboratory and going into trailer production. He displayed an updated model at the Detroit Auto Show in January 1930 and reportedly sold 118 trailers at the show at $400 each.

Detroit was an important hub for campers vacationing in the Great Lakes states. As the centre of the US automobile industry, it was also the ideal place to buy or make trailer parts. Based in Detroit, Sherman was the right man in the right place at the right time. Demand for the manufactured travel trailer took off right on his doorstep. During the 1930s a number of new Covered Wagon trailers were introduced, ranging from 16ft to 22ft in length and all reasonably priced. Covered Wagons were the first travel trailers to include electric brakes controlled from the tow

The first Covered Wagon by Arthur Sherman (USA, 1929)

vehicle as a standard accessory. They also featured in a number of road movies. Covered Wagon went on to become the largest trailer manufacturer in the USA during the 1930s. In 1937 *Fortune* magazine called the company 'the Ford of the trailer industry'. By 1938 Sherman was employing over 1,400 workers, producing 80 trailers a day and had sold 15,000 trailers to that date. In 1937 the company was hit by the recession and intense competition from other trailer manufacturers. The company made truck cargo bodies during the war but would never build trailers again, ceasing production in 1945.

At the start of the 1930s the growth of the RV industry attracted the attention of department store owner Sears, Roebuck and Company. 'The Split Coach is the greatest product ever given to Outdoor America', proclaimed a 1930 advert

somewhat immodestly as the company decided to build its own RV. The Split Coach derived its name from its patented trick of splitting open along its middle to allow the sides to slide out and the roof to be raised. As such it was one of the first RVs to feature a 'slide out' function using telescopic tubular steel poles to support the slide-out's floors. At the same time, it heralded the end of the 1920s tent trailer movement – the Split Coach was about as sophisticated as tent trailers could get without becoming fully enclosed.

The Split Coach was promoted as a way to 'obviate hotel bills and meals in restaurants'. It contained four berths, a refrigerator, room-dividing curtains, electric lighting and bathroom facilities. Large cupboards for fishing tackle, golf clubs, umbrellas and camping gear were provided. Tests

The Split Coach by Sears, Roebuck and Company (USA, 1930)

apparently showed that the trailer reduced the speed of the tow vehicle by 'only four miles an hour over good roads'. The Split Coach cost $875 in standard configuration and $1,250 for the deluxe model. These prices were high for a camper trailer, however elaborate, and would have been equivalent to or greater than the price of some of the fixed-wall trailers that were starting to appear on the market in the early 1930s.

Although Detroit was the logical place to manufacture RVs, it soon had a rival in the form of Elkhart, Indiana. Elkhart was no flash in the pan, since it is known today as the RV capital of the world, with over 80 per cent of global RV production now coming from this region. According to RV historian Al Hesselbart, Elkhart's claim to fame began in the 1930s, when three companies, Milo Miller's Sportsmen Trailers, Harold Platt's Platt Trailers and Wilbur Schult's Schult Trailer Coach began making travel trailers in large numbers. Their combined trailer output soon outgrew that of Michigan. Of these, Schult was the largest.

The travel trailer display at Chicago's 1933 World Exposition was the inspiration behind Wilbur Schult's move into the trailer business. With a loan from his mother, he started selling Covered Wagon and Sportsmen trailers on consignment from a new retail outlet called the Schult Trailer Mart. In 1936, Schult took over the manufacturing space of Miller's Sportsmen Trailers and renamed the business Schult Trailer Coach, starting a period of rapid growth and astute acquisitions that would lead Schult to overtake the Covered Wagon company as the world's largest trailer manufacturer by 1939. By this time Schult had expanded overseas, manufacturing trailers in Canada and New Zealand.

Schult focused on producing travel trailers that were simple and affordable. The Schult Sportsman of 1936 was an early example of the company's straightforward construction style, and this was carried forward into larger trailers between 1937 and 1940. Consumer choice was also important to the company – in 1939 alone ten new models were introduced.

A Schult Sportsman travel trailer (USA, 1936)

The Schult Continental Clipper (USA, 1939)

In 1938 Schult deviated from its traditional trailer business by building a custom, 40ft luxury trailer called the Continental Clipper for publisher Myron Zobel. The story of this RV is told in Zobel's 1955 book *The 14-Karat Trailer*, according to which 'the interior was panelled with Australian satinwood and figured aspen and the walls were of tufted pigskin'. The book provides a cautionary tale for anyone planning to order a custom-built trailer, which in Zobel's case was long delayed and went heavily over budget. It was later sold on to King Farouk of Egypt.

As war approached, Schult had the foresight to form good relationships with the US government. When war began, Schult, unlike most of its competitors, was able to continue trailer production by supplying the US Army with military equipment including military housing (including for workers on the Manhattan Project), prisoner-of-war transports, glider transport vehicles and even portable morgues. Thanks to its acquisitions, flexible approach and affordable products, the company was one of the few to survive the war. With a later focus on fixed mobile dwellings, the company continued under Schult's leadership until 1957, when it became Schult Homes.

Other Travel Trailer Manufacturers of the 1930s

Alongside trailer giants Covered Wagon and Schult were hundreds of smaller trailer manufacturers seeking to capitalise on the trailer boom of the early 1930s. By 1938 it was reported that there were as many as 400 trailer manufacturers operating in America. Mass manufacturing techniques invented by Henry Ford had made their way into the trailer industry, allowing the bigger manufacturers to produce hundreds of trailers each week. Materials were chosen on cost grounds rather than looks or durability. Some makers chose a leatherette material to cover their trailers which was attractive when new but not very durable.

The 'toaster' shape became the predominant look of 1930s American travel trailers. It was cheap to build, offered lots of internal space and provided good headroom. 'Toasters' were also easily adaptable to other uses such as mobile offices or product displays for travelling salesmen. The oval-shaped caravans of England were built in smaller quantities by some makers. They were called 'canned ham' trailers because their

Above left: An RV Sportsman trailer made from used automobile parts (USA, 1932)

Above middle: A travel trailer named by *The Caravan* magazine (UK) as 'The Doodlebug', possibly made by the Hollywood Trailer Company (USA, 1935)

Above right: A Deluxe Kauneel trailer in Bay City, Michigan (USA, 1936)

Above left: A Kabin Koach travel trailer (USA, 1936)

Above middle: A Palace Travel Coach (USA, 1936)

Above right: A York-Hoover Sun Chasr trailer (USA, 1936)

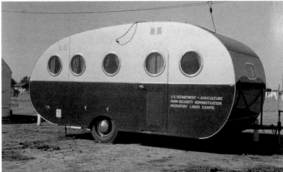

Above left: A Bender travel trailer (USA, c1936)

Above middle: An Airfloat trailer with its trademark round windows. This example was used in a California migratory labour camp of the Farm Security Administration (USA, 1939)

Above right: An Alma Silvermoon trailer. Oval-shaped trailers were known as 'canned ham' trailers in the USA (USA, 1938)

shape resembled a tin of ham and were regarded as small and quaint. The powerful tow vehicles being produced in America combined with Depression-era state highway building programs allowed American trailers to become large and often heavy. Employees of one trailer builder would sometimes leave to form a competing company. Although this led to intense competition, this would also mean limited variation in shape or size between manufacturers. There were exceptions of course, and a few American travel trailers of the period have since become RV design classics.

Manufacturers would compete to have their travel trailers featured in movies. Trailers provided storylines for a number of road trip movies and one appeared in a 1938 Mickey Mouse cartoon. Travel trailers also served as dressing rooms for Hollywood stars, with most of the major trailer manufacturers keen to have the stars of the day filmed using one of their trailers. Some stars would use these trailers for their own vacations.

It is not possible to feature all 400 or so American trailer manufacturers of the late 1930s in a curated history of this kind. A small sample is shown opposite.

The Teardrop Trailer

Whilst most of the American RV industry of the 1930s focused on large travel trailers, a new RV design emerged during this period that was tiny. The iconic small RV known as a teardrop trailer is commonly thought to have originated in California in the 1930s. Teardrops are defined by their shape, outside rear kitchen and internal sleeping area with low roof. Of their history, US RV historian Douglas Keister writes:

'Since most of these early teardrops were homebuilt, it's hard to plumb the exact date of the first true teardrop trailer... There is anecdotal information that some homebuilt teardrop trailers may have been made as early as 1933 or 1934. Throughout the late 1930s, handyman-oriented magazines were chock-full of a variety of plans for these tidy little trailers. Eventually companies started manufacturing ready-to-assemble kits and complete trailers.'

from *Teardrops and Tiny Trailers*
by Douglas Keister, 2008

A 'teardrop trailer' illustration appeared in *Popular Science* magazine in April 1936, closely followed by a design in the same publication for a motorcycle trailer from 'a German inventor' in June 1936. These were some of the earliest references to the teardrop. One of the earliest teardrops to go into production was the Kaycraft Kampster of Pasadena in California. Designed by Walter Hille and J.S. McBeth, trailer construction plans for this teardrop trailer appeared in the December 1936 and January 1937 issues of *Outdoor Life* magazine. Plans for another branded teardrop, the Runlight, appeared in *Motor Mechanix* in 1938.

There is also some early evidence of international interest in the teardrop. In France, a company called La Remorque Industrielle developed a small *couchette camping* or camping berth which it called La Baby. This teardrop-shaped camper was claimed to have been created in 1936, and some in France claim that the teardrop concept was developed there and exported to the USA. In Australia, the Caravan Construction and Hire Company built a Land Cruiser Sports Tourer teardrop in 1937. It had a swept-up rear end typical of many Australian RVs to facilitate creek crossings.

As with most RVs, the birth of the teardrop is likely to have been an evolution of designs from several sources. The year 1936 seems to be the year when the teardrop took off, and it probably did so in California. The climate would have lent itself well to the outdoor lifestyle required of teardrop owners, whilst its low price and relatively simple construction would have appealed to the many Californian migrants and self-builders of the 1930s.

A teardrop trailer at the sales yard of Halsco Land Yacht (USA, 1936)

The Streamliner – Brooks Stevens (1936)

'I believe in status symbols.'

Brooks Stevens

As the 1930s progressed, the popularity of RV streamlining gradually dwindled among the larger travel trailer manufacturers. A curved surface took longer to make and was more costly than a flat one, so it was left to high-end designers such as Brooks Stevens to take streamlining to its limits. Stevens was an iconic industrial designer responsible for some of the most aesthetically-pleasing vehicles and products ever seen. He and his staff designed over 3,000 products for 600 customers including machines, automobiles, locomotives – and RVs. Even though his RV designs were limited editions or one-offs for wealthy clients, their influence on contemporary and future generations of RV builders was profound.

His 1936 Zephyr Land Cruiser for millionaire Bill Plankinton was based on a Curtiss Aerocar and an International tractor. Stevens then received a design commission from the Western Printing Company to produce a number of small but beautifully-rounded sales vans in 1937. These in turn provided design inspiration for the Western Clipper, a housecar built

The Land Cruiser designed by Brooks Stevens for the Plankinton Company (USA, 1936)

for Herbert F. Johnson of SC Johnson Wax for use on research trips. A second housecar similar to the Western Clipper was built for W.M. Campbell of the Campbell Baking Company, which is reported to have been later modified by upholsterer Howdy Ledbetter into the Western Flyer in 1941. The interiors of Stevens' RVs were as refined as the exteriors – sleek, elegant and timeless. Even though Stevens coined the term 'planned obsolescence', his RV designs would be as much at home on today's roads as the day they were built.

A lesser-known 'streamliner' of the late 1930s was J. Roy Hunt. Hunt was a Hollywood cinematographer and was the director of cinematography on many movies including *Beau Geste*, *A Kiss for Cinderella* and *Flying Down to Rio*. To make life more comfortable whilst on location, in 1937 he purchased the chassis of a Ford truck and commissioned an auto-body specialist in Southern California to build a streamlined steel body with flush windows and doors. It was called the Hunt Housecar. The interior included a shower and folding toilet. Hunt went on to build a number of experimental housecars until his death in 1972. Hunt is today regarded by US RV enthusiasts as a pioneer of the streamlined RV movement.

'Gasoline Gypsies'

'People ought to have a home somewhere.'

President Franklin D. Roosevelt, 28 March 1939

During the 1930s unease grew around the number of Americans living permanently in trailers. Whilst estimates varied, it was said in 1938 that as many as 250,000 trailers were on American roads occupied by a million people. The US travel trailer industry estimated in 1939 that around ten per cent of new, commercially-manufactured trailers were being bought as full-time housing. Including self-built trailers there were accordingly about 75,000 trailers being used as full-time dwellings. One newspaper columnist of the time joked that soon half of America would be living in trailers.

Concerns over full-time trailer users centred around the non-payment of taxes, children's education (or lack of it) and crime. Terms such as 'gasoline gypsies' and 'auto tramps' that had been around since the early 1920s began to be used in the media in a more derogatory sense. The unhealthy state of some ad hoc

A squatter camp on the outskirts of Bakersfield, California (USA, 1936)

One of the many housecars under construction by homeless people in California in the mid-1930s (USA, 1935)

trailer parks and their impact on adjacent real estate values was widely reported upon.

In 1936 the Federal Government began attempts to regulate trailer parks, focusing on land use and using court cases to decide whether a trailer was a vehicle or a house. In response, trailer manufacturers set up an association to defend what they saw as an attack on their industry. The outcome was the introduction of a series of measures to regulate the industry. Restrictions were imposed on the length of stay in trailer parks, some imposing a period as short as 30 days. Trailer licensing fees were applied and national standards for trailer parks were introduced in 1939. Trailer dealers worked with the more reputable park operators to secure sites for their customers, and some became park owners.

Following these measures, by the end of the 1930s the trailer was seen as a recreational vehicle, not a permanent dwelling, and treated accordingly. It was somewhat ironic therefore, that by the time of America's entry into the Second World War in 1941, trailers were required by the Federal Government on a massive scale to provide medium-term housing for workers involved in war production and agriculture. As a result, instead of accounting for 10 per cent of production, trailers for long-term occupation accounted for 90 per cent of production by the early 1940s. This was the beginnings of the 'mobile home' concept that would create a new post-war industry in America.

Towards the end of the 1930s the American travel trailer boom turned to bust. Intense competition among manufacturers led to a massive oversupply of products. Attempts were made to create new overseas markets for American travel trailers through product licensing arrangements, but international demand for large, heavy trailers was limited. As war approached, most US travel trailer manufacturers would go out of business, and those that remained were required to produce low-cost trailers for the US government. The dreaming days for the trailer industry were very quickly over, and its few survivors would have to wait until the 1950s for US travel trailer manufacturing to experience a second boom. Today over 10 million American households own an RV, with about 10 per cent of those living in their RV full time. Due in large part to its good roads, beautiful places to visit, outstanding designers and efficient production facilities, America's love affair with the RV remains as strong as ever.

CHAPTER 5

GERMANY

"

The English-American caravans are certainly extremely comfortable, but they are heavy, unbelievably heavy. The people there have large tow vehicles and the money to tow these petrol-hungry machines. In Germany we have neither the money nor the time to meander slowly from one luxury resort to another. We must work, we have light cars and little time. We only have the weekends and a few days or weeks at the height of summer.

"

from *'Jachten der Landstraße'* by Hans Berger (1938)

A Dethleffs Tourist caravan (Germany, 1934)

Work before Leisure

Germany's contribution to the development of the RV in all its forms is a significant one. Perhaps best known internationally is the Volkswagen Kombi dating from 1950, an iconic motorhome which revolutionized holiday travel for millions of mainly young people. But Germany's involvement in RV design and manufacturing goes back much further. During the 1930s a small number of German caravan manufacturers defied the political, social and economic upheaval of the decade by making lightweight caravans with intelligent layouts that would influence the country's RV design direction for many decades. Three manufacturers in particular – Arist Dethleffs, Hans Berger and Wolf Hirth – were important pioneers in the construction of small caravans in the 1930s but are largely unknown outside Germany. International recognition of this influential group is long overdue.

Following the formation of the German Empire in 1871 there was a dramatic economic change across the country. Germany's transformation from a predominantly rural economy into a major industrial power was so successful that by 1914 it was the world's second largest economy after the USA. Rural workers had flocked to the new industrial centres around Berlin and the Ruhr Valley, working six days a week for poor pay and conditions and leaving little time or money available for recreation. It is no surprise then, that Germany was a latecomer in adopting the RV as a form of leisure transport.

Unlike Britain, France or the USA, there is scant evidence of Germans using horse-drawn caravans for leisure in the late 1800s or early 1900s, even amongst the wealthy. Tent camping was popular amongst the outdoor-minded, particularly in southern Germany with its outstanding forests and mountain scenery. Hans Berger, a German caravan manufacturer from Munich, wrote in 1938 that he was unable to say for sure who built the country's first leisure caravan. Before 1900, if caravans were seen on German roads at all, they tended to be those of circus folk, actors or artists. Roving circuses and seasonal fairs were two of the few forms of leisure enjoyed by an otherwise busy nation.

One notable German vehicle used as accommodation was the huge caravan of Hugo Haase, a Germany circus owner from Roßlau near Leipzig. Known as 'The King of the Roundabouts', Haase was a pioneer in the construction of large and complex amusement rides. As he toured Germany, Italy, Switzerland and Austria with his circus, he lived in this large three-roomed caravan deemed by the British press to be 'the most luxurious movable dwelling in existence'. It was lit

The large caravan of circus owner Hugo Haase (unknown location, c1900)

The 'drivable house' of landscape artist Hermann Kiekebusch (Germany, 1910)

by electricity and was fitted with coal fireplaces. A chef was employed to prepare meals for Haase and his guests using a separate kitchen caravan.

With the advent of the automobile, Germany joined France and the USA by producing touring limousines for the wealthy. The Benz Reisewagen of 1906 had a 40hp engine, body-hugging suitcases at the rear and allowed its occupants to sleep on two folding seats. In 1910, a German automobile newspaper showed a photograph of an early German motorhome, possibly Germany's first. It was a quirky but spacious RV that reflected the creative nature of its owner. It was called a 'drivable house' and belonged to a landscape artist from Coburg called Hermann Kiekebusch. His 'residence on wheels' consisted of a motor vehicle of unknown make with painted canvas walls that extended on both sides to create a lounge and a bedroom. There was a veranda at the rear and the central section contained another room, kitchen and bathroom. The furniture was collapsible, and the lighting was electric.

Post-War Austerity

During the First World War there are some records of wooden caravans belonging to the German creative community being used for military accommodation, but unlike some Allied nations there is little evidence of RVs being used in the early post-war years. The reason for this was clear – the collapse of the once great German economy. Already bankrupted by conflict, Germany was forced to pay heavy reparations to the Allies. The country remained impoverished throughout the 1920s and once again in no position to think of holidays or leisure. Still, circuses and fairs resumed their travels around the country on a limited scale, using residential caravans as part of a roving attraction.

First appearing in European newspapers in 1922, the *Villa Wandervogel* ('Rolling Stone Villa') was built by Austrian-born Franz von Schlechtleitner. He was reputed to have fallen on hard times after the First World War and decided to travel throughout Germany in a self-built vehicle reminiscent of a

The *Villa Wandervogel* of Franz von Schlechtleitner (Germany, 1922)

A slimmed-down *Villa* at the Berlin International Automobile Exhibition (Germany, 1931)

Bavarian farmhouse. Its primary purpose was to sell goods at local fairs, but it also contained accommodation. Its upper level balconies were adorned with flowers, there were antlers on the roof and the wheels were hidden by fabric. The main vehicle towed a secondary trailer that was similarly decorated.

A second, simplified version of this 'farmhouse on wheels' appeared in Berlin almost a decade later in 1931. The chassis had been updated or replaced, the trailer had disappeared, and painted bricks adorned the fabric covering the wheels. The publicity material associated with this photograph reads:

'A motorhome for travel, hunting and summer refreshment - the dream of every weekender. The home is firmly mounted on to the chassis of a truck. Height and width are in accordance with legal requirements. Patent owner: Franz von Schlechtheimer.'

The apparent name change is possibly a spelling error.

An interior photo of the 1931 villa suggests that selling goods on the road was no longer the primary purpose of the vehicle. Given that the vehicle was positioned in or near the Berlin Automobile Exhibition of that year, von Schlechtleitner was possibly seeking to find customers who would commission him to build a similar vehicle.

A German Motorhome of the 1920s

Despite the economic austerity of the 1920s, at least two well-known German manufacturers produced motorhomes for leisure purposes during this period. In 1928 German truck and bus manufacturer Büssing produced an unusual triple-axle motorhome, a passenger bus conversion about which little is known. In the same year, truck and bus manufacturer Maschinenfabrik Augsburg-Nürnberg AG, better known in the heavy goods vehicle world as MAN, produced a long, sumptuous and heavy motorhome called the *Wochenend Wagen* or Weekend Wagon. It was produced for Mitropa, the dining and sleeping car operating company of the German railways.

The Weekend Wagon was exhibited at the Berlin International Automobile Exhibition in 1928 and attracted much interest. It had a raised roof at the rear with upper windows for added light. The motorhome had an ash frame clad in thin sheet-iron and had a chauffeur's area, living room, bedroom, kitchen and washroom with toilet. Fitout included flush-mounted ash trays in folding tables, an electric cigar lighter, Caucasian walnut doors and walls, padded silk floral wall covering, silk curtains, electric ceiling and reading lights, frosted glass built in the interior door and bunks and folding ladders for four people. A Frigidaire fridge and Dutch oven complemented a stove in the kitchen whilst the bathroom had a shower and chemical toilet. There was a large water tank under the floor which used an electric pump to deliver water to the sink and shower. An extra folding bed was made available for a maid, whilst the chauffeur slept in the front driving compartment.

MAN's Weekend Wagon may have been intended for road use by wealthy clients of the German railways, but no photographic records have yet been discovered of the vehicle in use. Even so, it was a high-quality example of early German engineering and design in the motorhome field.

The MAN *Wochenendwagen* or Weekend Wagon (Germany, 1928)

Imports and Heavyweights

The New York stock market crash of 1929 heralded the Great Depression. Cash-starved Allies who had made loans to Germany in the 1920s sought early repayment. These economic shocks left the country on its knees, with a conservative estimate of nine million unemployed in 1933. Records exist of rudimentary caravans being hand-pulled by unemployed miners as they travelled in search of work. Yet again the country had more important issues to deal with than thinking about leisure. Nevertheless, it was during the early 1930s that a small number of German RV pioneers began to build caravans for leisure.

Around 1930 a trickle of British caravans was either imported into Germany or used by British holiday-makers for trips to Europe. A caravan appeared on the streets of Berlin with an accompanying sign that read in part, 'Weekender or hunting lodge on a trailer. Suitable to be towed by any car or motor bike. Caravans. First manufacturer in Germany'. Although it is possible this may have been a German self-built caravan, it is more likely to have been an English Eccles.

A self-built caravan was a more affordable way to take a holiday in difficult economic circumstances. In the spring and summer of 1934, Hamburg-based travel writer and journalist Heinrich Hauser took his family on a 143-day caravan trip through Germany in a large, self-built caravan. Hauser's four-wheeled caravan called the *Arche* ('Ark') became well known across the country thanks to Hauser's 1935 account of the journey called *Fahrten und Abenteuer im Wohnwagen* or 'Travels and Adventures in a Caravan'. The trip was something of a nightmare. Built largely of spare parts from other vehicles and painted in police vehicle colours to reduce suspicion, the *Arche* weighed 2 tonnes when loaded, making it difficult to control on Germany's narrow roads of the time. Frequent detours had to be made to avoid low bridges. Although Hauser's account increased public awareness of the possibilities of recreational caravan travel within Germany, his adventures also offered an early warning to potential caravan manufacturers of the dangers of building large, overweight caravans.

A caravan for sale on the streets of Berlin (Germany, 1930)

The Birth of The German Lightweight Caravan

Germany's caravan-building efforts of the 1930s were fragmented and highly localized. It was a cottage industry led by pioneers with expertise in other fields such as tent or glider making. But in a country where even a motorcycle was a luxury, these pioneers understood the importance of making caravans light enough to be towed by affordable automobiles. Germany's lightweight caravan movement, such as it was, began in 1931 in the country's south, a key tourist destination close to the European Alps.

Arist Dethleffs was a travelling service agent for his family's business in Isny, south-west of Munich, that manufactured horse whips and ski sticks. Dethleffs married in 1931, but his wife Fridel soon became uneasy about his long absences on the road. To overcome the problem, she suggested that her husband build for them 'something like a gypsy caravan that we can travel together in and I can paint in'. So in 1931, Dethleffs built his first *Wohnauto*, or caravan, to provide accommodation for his family on the road as well as a studio for Fridel. Dethleffs gave the caravan to his wife as a wedding present in 1932.

This was Germany's first-known, motor-drawn caravan. It was 4.4m long, 1.6m wide and 2.1m high with roof raised. It was simply fitted out with a seat that could be converted into a double bed as well as a bunk bed, table and shelves. It was thoughtfully built, providing ventilation without draughts, safe towing due to its light weight, pneumatic tyres, low centre of gravity and good headroom thanks to its elevating roof. A replica of the Dethleffs *Wohnauto* is part of the collection of the Erwin Hymer Museum, an RV museum in Bad Waldsee, Germany.

During business trips, Dethleffs would often be asked about his unusual vehicle. One curious onlooker thought it might be a hearse, but a more common reaction was to ask if it was available for purchase. In 1932 this positive feedback gave Dethleffs sufficient courage to start building caravans for clients in a shed on the family's business premises. Dethleffs continued to refine his *Wohnauto* into something more streamlined, and by 1934 prototypes of a new caravan called the Dethleffs *Tourist* caravan were complete. The new caravan included a hardwood frame, double panelling and was mounted on a tubular steel chassis with spring suspension. It also included the Dethleffs trademark – a roof that could be raised and lowered. Its biggest

The Dethleffs family with their *Wohnauto* caravan (Germany, c1934)

A Dethleffs *Tourist* caravan under construction, showing its lightweight frame (Germany, c1937)

asset however was its lightness – it weighed only 430kg and so could be towed safely by a wide range of automobiles.

There was sufficient interest in the *Tourist* to start limited production. By 1936 Dethleffs had a staff of six people producing a modest number of *Tourist* caravans each year. Dethleffs continued to be a successful RV producer after the Second World War and beyond and was eventually purchased by Hymer in 1983.

Another important German lightweight caravan pioneer was Munich-based Hans Berger, originally a designer and manufacturer of tents and folding boats. As a friend of writer Heinrich Hauser, Berger had learned of Hauser's experiences with his heavy, self-built caravan and took these lessons to heart. Any caravans that Berger built would be lightweight. Berger felt strongly that Germany had the potential to build better lightweight caravans than any other country because, in his words, 'Germany is the land of lightweight construction, associated low cost and basic research and has assumed world leadership in the related fields of glider, airship and folding kayak construction'.

In 1930, when on holiday with a Dutch friend who owned an English camper trailer, Berger began to consider how the trailer's design could be adapted for the German market. A keen camper since childhood, Berger had watched with interest as tents had grown from basic shelters to large outdoor homes. His camping customers asked if he could build them a tent trailer. He agreed in principle but would not do so until he felt he had the right design.

In 1934 Berger developed a lightweight, camper trailer prototype from folding kayak canvas and an old three-wheeled vehicle chassis, but he was not yet content. In 1935, after much trial and error, Berger felt that the third version of his trailer was good enough to go into production. It was called the *Haus Dabei* or 'House with You' and was, as far as we know, Germany's first RV to go into limited production. It was a folding tent trailer and weighed only 200kg. Glowing reports of this new type of camper trailer in the German press led to strong sales. The *Haus Dabei* was simple, efficient, lightweight, easy to tow and more comfortable than tent camping. It received particular praise for its ability to be towed easily up the steep, winding mountain roads of the German and Swiss Alps.

The *Haus Dabei* sold well, but also unleashed many requests from customers for a bigger and better caravan similar to those available overseas. Berger temporarily resisted the temptation to build a large caravan, and instead under his new *Sportberger* brand remained true to the small, solid-walled caravan that he felt better suited German roads and pockets. The *Kajüte* ('Cabin') was Berger's first 'full-sized' caravan built in 1937. It was a folding-roof model weighing only 280kg. It included a letterbox on the front door, perhaps hinting to his customers that they might like to enjoy longer holidays in Berger's caravans than they were normally accustomed to.

A Berger prototype caravan (Germany, 1934)

A Berger *Haus Dabei* camping trailer behind a Ford V8 Cabriolet (Switzerland, 1937)

After overseas trips to France and Holland to study the caravans of those countries, Berger succumbed to consumer pressure and developed a *Groß-Karawane* or 'Big Caravan'. But when customers saw it up close, they felt that its length of 4.6m and weight of 650kg was too great and sales failed to take off.

Berger's biggest pre-war hit was neither large nor small, but just right. Called simply the *Sportberger Karawane*, or Sportberger Caravan, it was launched in 1939. It was 3.9 metres long and weighed 430kg. Its headroom was 1.82 metres and it could accommodate two people comfortably and four at a pinch with folding beds. Most importantly, it could be towed by less powerful cars along Germany's most demanding mountain roads. There were a few reports of piston seizures in less powerful tow vehicles when towing it at the height of summer, but overall the caravan was a success. Just before the start of the Second World War, Berger's caravan factory was producing one Sportberger Caravan a day and employed eighty workers. After the war Berger continued to produce caravans and camping equipment into the 1960s.

A third lightweight caravan pioneer of the 1930s was racing driver, glider pilot and aircraft designer Wolf Hirth from Kirchheim in southern Germany. Hirth had a passion for glider flying and design, something he had in common with US aircraft and RV builder Hawley Bowlus (see page 133). In 1931 the two formed a partnership to create a glider training school called the Bowlus-Hirth Soaring School in New York. Both Bowlus and Hirth were aware of the importance of aerodynamics to RV design. This is how Hirth explained the relevance of aircraft design to caravan manufacturing in a 1938 brochure:

'Why aircraft engineers can build high quality caravans:

1. **Light Construction:** important for aircraft climbing power and for automobile and caravan combinations
2. **Aerodynamic Form:** to increase speed and reduce fuel consumption
3. **Ingenious Use of Space:** every space and every kilogramme must have a practical and useful purpose
4. **A Chassis with high cross-country mobility:** important for both aircraft and caravans.'

A Berger *Karawane* caravan (Germany, c1938)

The *Aero-Sport* by Wolf Hirth (Germany, 1938)

Hirth introduced a number of design innovations into his caravans including monocoque construction, independent suspension and aircraft-inspired aerodynamic design. Other intelligent design features included double-wall insulation, rounded floor to wall junctions for easier cleaning and a flap and vents for the internal cooking area to reduce smells. A double bed and table combination was adjustable to allow simultaneous sitting and sleeping. There was even an optional front flap for storing kayaks inside the van during travel. Hirth seems to be the first caravan manufacturer anywhere to offer to fit identical wheels to the caravan and tow vehicle, reducing the number of spare wheels to be carried. The *Aero-Sport* weighed only 330kg, was 4.27m long and 2.14m high. During 1938 Hirth built a total of 30 caravans.

Hirth continued caravan production after the Second World War with a model called the *Tramp*. His life story is told in a biography by Karl Buck.

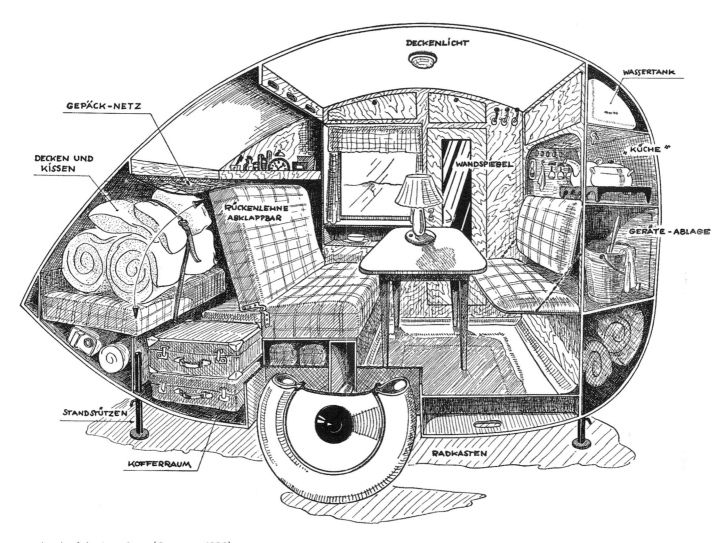

A cutaway sketch of the *Aero-Sport* (Germany, 1938)

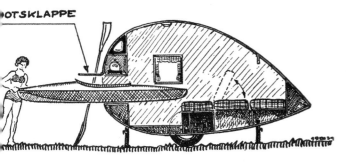

A diagram from the *Aero-Sport* brochure showing an optional front flap on the *Aero-Sport* to allow kayaks to be stored inside the van during travel (Germany, 1938)

Schlechte Umströmung!

Aero-Sport-Stromlinie!

A diagram from the *Aero-Sport* brochure showing the effects of wind resistance on conventional and aerodynamic vans (Germany, 1938)

A Caravan in Africa

'We want to spend our lives not in luxury hotels, but outside in the bosom of nature, where the jackal howls and where there are no superiors in tailcoats.'

Theo Rockenfeller

Theo Rockenfeller's Sportberger *Karawane* surrounded by sheep in Africa (Libya, 1938)

Berlin travel writer and journalist Theo Rockenfeller was a strong believer in independent travel. He often encouraged Germans to take their holidays in natural surroundings away from hotels. In 1938 he set an example to his readers by undertaking a caravan trip from Berlin to Libya with his wife, writer Ilse Lundberg. Rockenfeller's accounts, photographs and films of his journey created great interest in caravan holidays in Germany. On his return, public slide shows of his travels were often sold out.

Rockenfeller's tow vehicle of choice for Africa was a Ford V8 cabriolet and his caravan was a Sportberger *Karawane*. Prior to his trip Rockenfeller had tested a *Karawane* in Berlin and found it ideal for his needs. When Rockenfeller arrived in Africa he was surprised at the level of interest the caravan generated, with crowds flocking around the vehicle everywhere they went. They had colourful encounters with villagers, sheiks, a princess and no small numbers of camels and sheep. The Rockenfellers spent five weeks away, covering 3,650km on land and spending every night but one in the caravan. Both automobile and caravan performed flawlessly. For the Rockenfellers the holiday was a dream realized, and in the minds of many of Rockenfeller's readers and audience members it planted the idea of taking their first caravan trip.

RV Growth and Regulation

As well as the pioneering RV design work carried out in the 1930s by Dethleffs, Berger and Hirth, a number of other German RV manufacturers tried their hand at small-scale caravan manufacturing including Westfalia, Schweikert, Keutgen and Budich. In 1938 Westfalia conducted a high profile but short-lived experiment with a large travel trailer called the *Landstreicher*, based on a design from the USA's Covered Wagon. It was certainly luxurious but too big and heavy for most German tastes. Resisting external influences, German caravans of this period instead took on their own shape and character – streamlined, egg-shaped, often with a raised roof and always short and lightweight. By the late 1930s, thousands of Germans had purchased their first caravan. Trips were generally short and seasonal, but the hobby grew significantly in popularity.

In October 1938 Germany became one of the first countries to introduce construction regulations for caravans. The risks involved in towing an overweight caravan with an underweight automobile would have been familiar to world-class German vehicle engineers, so it was not unreasonable to set out clear rules for the construction of 'single axle trailers'. But these rules also increased construction costs and forced some of the smaller makers out of business.

As the Second World War approached, all manufacturers were required to divert their efforts to military production or stop manufacturing altogether. After the war, RV manufacturing would be left in the hands of a few large German manufacturers such as Dethleffs, Hymer, Volkswagen, Westfalia and Tabbert. Some of these companies would become household RV names around the world into the 1950s and beyond. They would all doubtless be quick to acknowledge the debt they owe to the country's pre-war RV pioneers, whose most significant legacy was perhaps the strong, safe, lightweight and aerodynamic German caravan.

CHAPTER 6

AUSTRALIA

> " Southern builders alone have made hundreds of caravans for the coming holidays, and hire caravans – for they can be rented like a house – are ten times too few to meet demand. Those who are not going in a caravan would like to be going. For caravans, like ships, appeal to the childish delight in 'cubby houses', in miniature and make-believe; and they please a more mature sense of ingenuity with their amazing combination of all essentials and luxuries in a space which, from the outside, looks ridiculously inadequate. "

The *Border Star*, Queensland, 30 September 1938

Opposite: The campsite of artist Bill Pidgeon with his Jennison Cruiser caravan at Bylong Valley Way, New South Wales (Australia, 1937)

The Horse-Drawn Caravan Era

Australia's open, diverse and generally flat landscapes combined with a relatively benign climate make it ideal for RV use. RVs are an extremely popular form of leisure in Australia today, with the country having the largest number of RVs per head of population in the world. But it was not always so.

Prior to European settlement in 1788, the Indigenous people who inhabited the Australian continent understood the land intimately. This was not the case for the first European migrants, in particular ill-qualified convicts, who tried and repeatedly failed to farm the land using inappropriate western methods, crops and animals. In the early to mid-nineteenth century, new arrivals to Australia therefore saw the continent as hostile, focusing more on survival than leisure. The country had no road networks to speak of outside the early migrant settlements. The dirt tracks that did exist were used by intrepid explorers, settlers, miners and hunters and were regularly exposed to the ravages of drought, flood and bush fires. Distances were vast and accommodation sparse, so the use of makeshift accommodation was common. Travellers slept in or under wagons or under the stars with a swag. When the Australian gold rushes began in the 1850s,

tents were the main form of shelter for gold miners, making camping a commonplace activity across the gold fields. Early Australian immigrant settlements, which later became towns, began as tented communities.

Land was often sold to settlers based on occupancy. Those claiming land rights were called 'squatters' and later 'selectors'. As this practise grew, so-called 'dummy selectors' would seek to accumulate multiple plots of land, moving from site to site and staying just long enough in each place to gain permission to make improvements before moving on. Basic 'houses on wheels' were sometimes used by these dummy selectors as temporary residences to prove occupancy. Later in the nineteenth century as European-style agriculture eventually became established and sheep and cattle farming began to prosper, drovers roamed the country, camping under the stars along the way. Agricultural shows, first held in Hobart in Tasmania in 1822 and now an established Australian tradition, would attract exhibitors from surrounding areas who often camped in tents close to their animals.

Leisure camping seems to have grown in popularity from the 1880s onwards, but nearly always close to towns, cities or the coast. The outback was perceived by many as the domain of bushrangers until Ned Kelly's death in 1880, so coastal settlers were in no hurry to make non-essential trips to the interior. In the early twentieth century, however, a few pioneering travellers took horse-drawn wagons on trips in order to explore, paint or see Australian nature close up.

One of the first Australians to use a horse-drawn wagon for leisure purposes was Frank Styant Browne. A Tasmanian-based pharmacist, photographer and painter, Styant Browne established the Northern Tasmanian Camera Club in 1889 and helped to introduce X-rays into Tasmania. In 1896 and 1899 he undertook two caravan trips to photograph the Tasmanian countryside along with artist Joshua Higgs.

Styant Browne's expeditions are reminiscent of photographer Roger Fenton's travels in the Crimea (see page 18), albeit under more peaceful circumstances. Whilst these trips were perhaps working holidays for Styant Browne, they took place at an idyllic period in Tasmania's history and provide a valuable glimpse of the early Australian horse-drawn leisure caravan. These trips are recorded in a book containing Styant Browne's diary and photos called *Voyages in a Caravan*, published in 2002 by Launceston Library.

In 1907 an ambitious journey was carried out by Australian poet and writer Edwin James Brady. He published a book in 1911 about his travels in a caravan called *The King's Caravan*. Accompanied by his companion Joe, Brady travelled

The McDonald family on a camping trip in the Yan Yean district of Victoria (Australia, c1905)

Above: Frank Styant Browne painting in Tasmania (Australia, either 1896 or 1899)

Right: *The King's Caravan* (Australia, 1907)

from Parramatta near Sydney to Townsville in Queensland, a distance of over 2,000kms. *The King's Caravan* of the title was a comical name given to the van by a friend before its departure.

'All the life I had lived was behind, and all the world before me. The wagon, which I already began to love, was my home. It contained all the potentialities of sport, of adventure, of novelty, and romance.'

from *The King's Caravan* by
E.J. Brady (1911)

Brady's trip was a major undertaking in 1907, financed by writing regular newspaper columns during the journey. His book provides a perceptive insight into rural Australia at the time as well as its people and abundant wildlife. Whilst Brady's caravan was perhaps unremarkable, his writings are those of an early travelling philosopher.

A caravanning venture with an environmental goal took place a year later in 1908. It was undertaken by Romeo Lahey, an Australian conservationist. His conservation campaigning led to the creation of Lamington National Park in Queensland in 1915. Lahey went on to found the National Parks Association of Queensland in 1930. Lahey's 'caravan' appears to be nothing more than a shed placed on top of a bullock cart, but it demonstrates the pragmatism of early self-builders.

Australian naturalist and writer Charles Leslie Barrett was another traveller with a purpose. He was a prodigious author, writing over fifty books and articles on wildlife, ornithology, lepidoptery and reptiles, and in later years covered the subject of Australian road tourism. His early travels were in a caravan. In a 1912 article called *The Open Road - The Joys of a Cruise in a Caravan*, Barrett described and pictured his own caravan. He explained the process of 'outspanning', the equivalent of erecting today's caravan awning. Four wooden slats, stored on the sides of the caravan during travel, were extended forwards and backwards, supported with vertical wooden posts and covered in canvas. The front canvas 'room' was used as a kitchen.

Short camping trips in horse-drawn caravans increased in popularity in the years before the First World War. The

Romeo Lahey's caravan (Australia, 1908)

Charles Barrett's caravan (Australia, 1911)

combination of long distances between towns and poor roads meant that extended leisure trips were not a practical option. Mobile accommodation for work purposes was more likely to be seen on Australian roads than camping wagons. In the late nineteenth century there are accounts of those building the first Australian railways and roads using living vans (see pages 18-19) as remote accommodation. Some agricultural workers were given onsite accommodation in the form of huts on wheels by the more foresighted farmers. But there was to be little progress in leisure caravanning until the advent of motorized transport.

The Motorized Era

When the automobile arrived in Australia in the early 1900s, it brought a dramatic transformation to industry, agriculture and communications across the country. Using automobiles for leisure was not uppermost in the minds of their lucky owners however, and the recreational potential of automobiles was not fully explored until the 1920s.

There were frequent reports in Australian newspapers of the popularity of RVs in the UK and USA from the early 1900s, so why was Australia a relatively late RV adopter? Australian newspapers of the time had plenty of theories. The *Australian Star* of June 1908 blamed the lack of local interest in caravanning on the absence of 'billiard table roads' common

in England. The *Queensland Figaro* of 25 June 1908 offered a tongue-in-cheek explanation as to why caravans were not popular in Australia:

> 'We fail to see any advantage in this form of locomotion [caravans]. It is certainly not speedy or comfortable or invigorating. There must be constant difficulties in obtaining the permission of farmers to desecrate their fields, tramps must be a frequent worry and the presence or absence of servants must be a perpetual irritation.'

Other reasons given by newspaper commentators included high cost, preference for hotels, reluctance to do household chores whilst on holiday and even 'a lack of that gypsy blood that gives the road its lure'. The most likely causes of the limited early take-up of leisure caravanning were poor roads, long distances and a lack of easily accessible tourist destinations.

But catch the RV bug Australia eventually did. After the First World War Australia's growing road network played host to a small number of motorhomes. The 'camping body' (automobiles adapted for camping) was a cost-effective means of taking a motoring holiday and these grew in popularity during the 1920s and 30s. In the late 1920s came the tent trailer and finally, in the early to mid-1930s, came the full height, solid-walled caravan.

An early caravan and tent holiday in South Australia (Australia, 1929)

The Graham Dodge motorhome of Dr. G. Craig (Australia, 1926)

The large distances between Australian towns and cities were a major handicap for horse-drawn transport, so the automobile and its truck-based derivatives were warmly welcomed in Australia. The first Australian motorhomes of the 1920s were basic, uncomfortable and often self-built by mavericks and DIY-enthusiasts. Few details of these motorhomes were made available in newspapers beyond a grainy photograph and a short caption.

Most motorhomes were converted from trucks or other vehicles. The 1923 Buick motorhome of Anthony Cummings, for example, was a converted ambulance. Dr Pockley's Ford motorhome of the same year was more ambitious, with a raisable roof to accommodate extra beds. The 1926 Graham Dodge motorhome belonging to Dr Gordon Craig also had a roof that could be raised, providing accommodation for four people. Early motorhome builders were quick to realize the need for these vehicles to navigate Australia's poor roads and shallow rivers, so included the large wheels, good ground clearance and rear cutaways that are common on many of Australia's 'off road' RVs today. Adaptations to Australian conditions were starting to become apparent.

In 1925 a South Australian Chevrolet dealer, Mann's Motors Limited, decided to hold a public competition to design a motorhome suited to local conditions. The prize of ten guineas and a two-week holiday in the motorhome attracted many entries and was won by a Mr A. Ridge. When the motorhome was finished, Ridge apparently enjoyed his touring holiday despite the significant attention his vehicle received. On his departure a gramophone was proudly played from within the motorhome to demonstrate its smooth suspension.

Towards the end of the 1920s motorhome standards began to improve. An example of a high-quality motorhome of this period is the 1929 Land Yacht constructed by Olsen and Goodchap, furniture makers from Brisbane. Built on a Reo chassis, the interior was luxuriously finished in Queensland maple with bevelled windows, brass washbasin, four drop-down berths, gold-plush curtains and a radio. Twin 20-gallon water tanks located on the roof would not have been beneficial to the vehicle's stability but apparently assisted with cooling the interior. A notable external feature was the dual awnings, significantly extending the private space of its occupants. The Land Yacht was used by both the Olsen and Goodchap families for holidays into the 1940s.

Perhaps the best-known Australian motorhomes of this period belonged to Gerhard 'Pop' Kaesler from South Australia. Kaesler's two self-built motorhomes of 1929 and 1932 were seen and admired by many on their travels. Whilst we now know that they were not, as sometimes claimed, Australia's first, they were early, eye-catching adverts for the RV lifestyle.

The Land Yacht constructed by Olsen and Goodchap of Brisbane, Queensland (Australia, 1929)

Kaesler, a South Australian coachbuilder and blacksmith, was typical of early RV pioneers worldwide – an 'outside the square' thinker. He built a pedal car for his children, a water-driven generator for his home, a water-powered washing machine, a box camera and a lathe. Significantly to many Australians, he also developed a prototype of the rotary clothesline that later became known as the 'Hills Hoist'.

In 1929, dissatisfied with the quality of hotels his family frequented whilst on holiday, he set about building a motorhome. Built on the chassis of a 1924 Dodge Tourer, Kaesler named it the *Home from Home*. It was quite literally a house on wheels, complete with pitched roof, chimney, gutters, brick cladding, windows, curtains and door. Roof gutters were installed and used to channel water into a barrel to provide water. The interior was less elaborate, with simple camping equipment and beds. Kaesler felt that the 'box on wheels' approach of other self-built motorhome builders was inadequate, and that nothing but the best for his family would do. He was so successful in this aim that on his first holiday with the motorhome he sold it to the Mayor of the South Australian town of Goolwa, who arranged for Kaesler and his family to return home without their *Home from Home*.

To celebrate his silver wedding, Kaesler built a second motorhome in 1931-32 called *The Cottage*. As well as his

trademark pitched roof and chimney, Kaesler added stained glass windows, imitation stone cladding, a folding sofa bed and even a chess board toilet lid. He fitted 12-gallon water tanks and two petrol tanks as insurance against the unreliable fuel supplies of the time. The Kaesler family took their second motorhome on holiday to outback New South Wales and Queensland, and whilst visiting Canberra gave Australia's Prime Minister Scullin a tour of the motorhome, followed by a family picnic on the lawns of Parliament House. *Home from Home* remains on display today in Goolwa, whilst *The Cottage* is on display at Kaesler's home town of Nurioopta, South Australia.

Despite the efforts of these early pioneers, the first Australian motorhomes were generally heavy and fuel-hungry. They would continue to be a niche RV product until well after the Second World War.

Australian Camper Trailers

Prior to the arrival of the Australian full height, solid-walled caravan, a small number of camper trailers appeared from around 1927. These were made by individual builders, coachbuilders or commercial trailer makers and were ideal for towing behind low-powered but affordable tow vehicles. One such vehicle was a canvas-covered trailer built in 1927 in Tasmania. It was built by a boat builder for the Bailey family, sheep farmers in Tasmania's mid-north. Unsurprisingly, the trailer's timber frame was similar to that used on wooden boats of the period, with waterproof canvas stretched over the frame. The interior was simply furnished and contained three beds, a folding table and folding seat. It was apparently used for local fishing and camping trips.

Also in 1927 a Mr Cooper of Ryde in Sydney built an elaborate camper trailer out of aluminium, reportedly in order to withstand the wear and tear of the road. It measured 8ft long by 6ft wide. The trailer formed a single 'room' when in tow, but when connected with multiple awnings at its destination created four additional spaces. The trailer could apparently be towed safely at up to 25mph. Another camper trailer builder, E.J. Boxer of Adelaide, South Australia, deserves a special mention for building in 1928 a trailer with a roof that could float. The trailer could apparently be assembled in ten minutes, accommodated three people and weighed 400kg. According to the *Adelaide Mail*, the roof, when removed, 'may be used on the water as a fishing skiff and accommodate four people with safety'. The *Mail* added that the appearance of the caravan at various resorts caused much interest.

Gerhard 'Pop' Kaesler's first motorhome known as *Home from Home* (Australia, 1929)

The Folding Fly-Proof Caravan of artist Hans Heysen with a Model A Ford in the Flinders Ranges, South Australia (Australia, 1932)

Perhaps the most iconic of early Australian camper trailers was The Folding Fly-Proof Caravan made by South Australian coachbuilders Eicke and Provis. Built to a patented folding design of Adelaide-based solicitor W. Ashley Norman from about 1930 onwards, this simple but effective camper trailer was canvas-topped and had a fly mesh screen for good ventilation and to keep out insects. Norman created a business called Trailer Caravans Ltd. and hired out these camper trailers under the Aero brand in the early 1930s. A modified version with a hard-top roof was also patented and introduced in 1936.

The Folding Fly-Proof Caravan came to fame when it was used by Australian landscape painter Hans Heysen for a painting expedition in 1932. Heysen was renowned for his paintings of the Flinders Ranges in South Australia. In 1931 he bought a Folding Fly-Proof Caravan and in March 1932 left with his son David on a month-long painting trip to Brachina Creek, Aroona. Heyson's biographer Colin Thiele reports that 'apart from minor mishaps with wheels and springs', the journey was uneventful. On arrival David erected a 45ft radio mast so that father and son could keep in touch with events elsewhere in Australia. When no longer required for travel, Heysen's trailer later served as an aviary.

Australian Caravans of the 1930s

The Folding Fly-Proof Caravan was suited to camping in the arid zones of central Australia as well as its tropical north. But Australia's southerners had to contend with a colder climate and required a more robust solution. So it was that the 1930s became the decade of the caravan. Reports of solid-walled, fixed-roof, motor-drawn caravans began to appear in the Australian press in the early 1930s. Early examples were generally one-off vehicles made for sale or hire by a local coachbuilder or garage.

Evidence of early Australian caravan manufacture is sketchy and, according to caravan historian Richard Dickins, blurred by some manufacturers claiming to have begun caravan manufacture at a period in their history when they were in fact building something else. A few self-builders became low-volume manufacturers when others saw their prototypes and decided they wanted one too. Early growth of the Australian caravan industry was sporadic and highly localized, with Dickins identifying a number of regionally specific design styles. South Australia (Adelaide) was probably the first region to build caravans on a limited scale followed by Victoria (Melbourne) and New South Wales (Sydney).

A few UK caravans, primarily those built by Eccles, reached Australia in the late 1920s and early '30s, usually

as the personal imports of new migrants. Along with press reports and photographs of caravans on British roads, these influenced early Australian caravan design. But the unsuitability of English caravans to Australian conditions soon became apparent. They had limited ground clearance, were too heavy, lacked adequate ventilation and had inadequate water storage for long-distance travel.

From the early 1930s onwards, Australian caravans began to assume their own unique features. These included streamlined bodies to reduce fuel costs over long distances, good ventilation, small windows to keep out the heat, high ground clearance for crossing rivers and sand dunes and cream-coloured exteriors to reduce heat absorption without the glare of white paint. The 'pop-top' caravan was an important design offshoot in Australia. It had a raisable roof which reduced wind resistance when on tow whilst providing extra headroom and ventilation at camp. The local version of the pop-top was probably pioneered by John Jennison in 1933. So-called 'caravanettes' – small caravans with a bed and an exterior kitchen – were also built in limited numbers.

One locally built but British-influenced caravan was made in 1932 by the Tivoli Garage in Perth. It is similar in design to British caravans of the late 1920s, notably those manufactured

A caravan made by the Tivoli Garage in Perth, Western Australia (Australia, 1932)

by Eccles. Perth's residents, many of whom were British expatriates, would have followed European motoring and leisure developments closely. Little is known about the Tivoli caravan, except that advertisements appeared in local newspapers explaining it was available for hire. Locals seem to have reacted with caution however, since there are no signs of it having been widely used.

A caravan builder who may have been Australia's first to start caravan manufacturing on a limited scale was W.H. Willshire of Adelaide. In early 1932 he built at least one and possibly two caravans in his spare time whilst working as a night watchman at the local abattoir. Like the Tivoli caravan, these caravans followed the UK Eccles design. One was exhibited at the Royal Adelaide Show of 1932. There was sufficient interest in Willshire's caravans to go into small scale manufacturing, and towards the end of 1933 he launched what one local newspaper called 'the Famous Paramount Streamline Trailer Caravan'. Later to become known just as Paramount Caravans, these were oval-shaped, similar in appearance to UK Winchester caravans, and were produced in three different sizes.

Willshire was a keen follower of UK caravan trends. Reports of his caravans appeared in the UK's *Caravan* magazine in 1934 and 1935. He also received a patent for a floor-lowering mechanism. Sales continued at a modest level until 1938 when Paramount Caravans went bankrupt. It is likely that the company fell victim to intense competition from larger Australian caravan manufacturers in the late 1930s.

Another early Australian caravan builder was George Moreland's Windmill Car Trailer Company. The company was based in Melbourne and claimed to have been in the caravan business since 1923. However, Richard Dickins believes this date probably referred to the manufacturing of other Windmill products such as luggage or tent trailers, and that caravan production only commenced in the early 1930s. Windmill advertised that they would build caravans to order from late 1932, just a few months after Willshire of Paramount, but no Windmill caravans of that period have yet come to light.

By 1937 Windmill was producing a staggering thirty-four different caravan models including the Swallow and the Moreland Cruiser. Windmill caravans had a contemporary design and included multiple roof hatches, wide front windows and even baths in some models. One of their slogans was 'half the weight of others and 75 per cent less in selling price'. Perhaps unsurprisingly then, Windmill went into liquidation in 1940. Moreland started making caravans again under his own name in the 1950s.

One of the first caravans constructed by W.H. Willshire of Adelaide, South Australia (Australia, 1932)

A Paramount caravan 'fording a billabong' appeared in the UK *Caravan* magazine of April 1935 (Australia, 1935)

A Windmill Swallow caravan at Kyneton in Victoria (Australia, c1935)

Australia was badly hit by the Great Depression, with unemployment reaching about thirty per cent in 1932. With Australia's main wool export markets similarly affected, it was left to the local manufacturing industry to restore jobs and wealth. Most of these manufacturers were located in New South Wales and Victoria, where caravan manufacturing played its part. In the mid-1930s, Melbourne in particular was becoming a hub for caravan builders.

One of the most renowned of the early Melbourne-based caravan manufacturers was Don Caravans, which manufactured caravans from 1934 until the 1960s. In notes accompanying one of the earliest-known photographs of a Don caravan, the State Library of Victoria comments that the Don Caravan was 'the first Australian made and designed caravan - it was designed especially for local conditions'.

Very much a family affair, Don Caravans was founded by Don Robinson in association with his father Richard ('Dick') Henry Robinson. Don was responsible for design, and brother Syd joined the company after the Second World War to look after sales and marketing. Dick Robinson's main business was automobiles but he was also a keen tent camper and fisherman. He would often have his camping trip spoiled by bad weather, so Don took pity on him and built him a caravan. Don used his interest in aviation to design a lightweight, streamlined caravan that would become the hallmark of the company's future products. Before the caravan was complete, it was sold to a customer willing to pay a good price for it. Other clients followed, and the company went into production using skilled craftsmen and traditional assembly methods.

The Rayner Sisters

'We go where we please and we envy nobody.'

Joan and Betty Rayner, 1935

Above left: Joan (left) and Betty Rayner with their Car Cruiser caravan in front of an English country estate during a UK tour (UK, 1930s)

Above right: Joan and Betty Rayner's Car Cruiser caravan being craned onto a ship during their European travels (Europe, 1930s)

New Zealanders Joan and Betty Rayner had a small, one-off caravan built for them in Sydney in 1929. The two sisters described themselves as 'troubadours'. After studying drama in the UK, they moved to Australia in 1920 and in 1929 established the Theatre of Youth in Sydney. Over the following forty-two years to 1971, they would travel extensively, both domestically and internationally, offering stories, plays and songs mainly for children through their Australian Children's Theatre. They focused on the small towns and rural areas of each country they visited as well as the Indigenous communities of Australia.

During their travels they lived in nine different caravans or motorhomes and generated significant interest not only in their performances, but also their recreational vehicles. In that sense they were RV ambassadors. On their retirement it was believed that they had performed to over two million children. Both were made Members of the Order of Australia in 1978.

A Rugby 6 car and Don 10-foot caravan (Australia, 1938)

Promoted as 'The Caravan for the Connoisseur', Don Caravans were highly regarded in their day. The characteristics that made them especially valued included light weight, a welded steel chassis, a wide wheelbase to reduce sway, leadlight windows, fly screens, chintz curtains and parchment light shades. Pre-war models were 10, 12 and 14ft in length, with customary paintwork being a cream upper half and green or blue lower half. The largest model was fitted with a bath and drop-down wash basin. Customer service was a high priority, with buyers encouraged to visit the factory to see their caravans being built. In 1938 and 1939 Dick Robinson made two trips from Melbourne to North Queensland to test their caravan in harsh conditions and to promote Queensland as a winter caravan destination.

A person who made a significant impact on Australian caravan building of the 1930s was John Jennison. Jennison was both a designer and an engineer with interests in caravans,

speedboats and racing cars. He built his first caravan in Salisbury, South Australia in the early 1930s before moving to Sydney in 1935, attracted by a larger potential market. His products were purpose-built for Australian conditions and included significant technical innovations. His first caravan design in the early years of the decade was small and oval-shaped, but he soon recognized that to build anything much larger would present wind resistance problems when towed by the ever-faster automobiles of the day. Jennison therefore designed a caravan with a roof that could be raised on arrival but kept the profile of the caravan low whilst under tow. This early 'pop-top' caravan appeared on the market in 1933 as the Jennison Cruiser. Jennison applied for a patent for his roof-raising mechanism in 1935.

Jennison went on to build non-pop-top caravans in the late 1930s under the Road Cruiser name, each one featuring

Above: A Jennison Cruiser pop-top caravan with John Jennison seated on the right with his eldest daughter Betty (centre) and son John (left) (Australia, 1935)

Below: A Traveluxe collapsible caravan (Australia, 1938)

a signature stripe on the side. These included lantern roofs and Masonite panelling. As well as mass producing caravans, Jennison also built them to order. One such example was the '*Wildeshott*' caravan built for Mr and Mrs Coles in about 1938 to the customer's design. Coles was a hunter and fisherman and used the caravan for his fishing trips within Australia including to Tasmania. The caravan featured a stuffed tiger's head on the wall – apparently the first of thirty tigers shot by Coles in India.

One of the larger caravan manufacturers to operate prior to the Second World War was the Melbourne-based Caravan Construction and Hire Company. They produced a range of caravans from around 1934 under the Land Cruiser brand, ranging from a small Sports Tourer 'teardrop' in 1937 to a luxurious Queen of The Road in 1938. The company did not re-appear after the war. Other notable Australian caravan manufacturers of the mid to late 1930s were Wolfenden Highway Homes and Windsor of Melbourne, Furness of Adelaide, Nomad and Brindle Caravans of Sydney and Queensland-based

Above: Caravans under construction at artist Byram Mansell's studio in Sydney. The caravans are probably Mobile Home caravans being built by Tom Propert & Son for Caravan Park (Australia, 1937)

Left: A Model T Ford converted for camping (known as a 'camping body') by Propert's Motor Body Company (Australia, 1922)

Traveluxe. Traveluxe built a range of caravans including a collapsible van well suited to the local climate.

Two Australian RV companies, Propert and Caravan Park, are best known to Australian RV enthusiasts for their post-1945 caravans. Less well known is their interwoven pre-1939 history and in particular the significant contribution of the Propert family to Australian caravan design and manufacturing of the late 1930s. Their early stories are best told as one.

Brothers Alf and Tom Propert were Sydney-based coachbuilders, establishing the Propert Body Works Company in about 1910. As well as building bodies for automobiles, buses and trucks, the company also built 'camping bodies'. This involved installing seats in automobiles that could be folded flat for sleeping (patented by Alf Propert in 1923) as well as a range

of camping storage compartments. Camping bodies allowed those on limited budgets to go camping using everyday vehicles.

In 1935 Tom Propert left the family business to set up his own motor body works business. Both Alf and Tom then separately considered how they could take advantage of the growing popularity of caravanning. They both did so in quite different ways. Tom formed a collaboration with a former car salesman, whilst Alf built his own caravans.

Tom's new caravan collaborator was R.J. Rankin. In the early 1930s Rankin had worked as an automobile salesman for Singer. Rankin and Alf Propert were both members of the Singer Car Club, which is where they may have first met. After Rankin's automobile sales partnership ended in late 1933, Rankin established his own automobile dealership based at the Propert Body Works premises at King Street, Newtown in Sydney in late 1934. A year or so after Tom Propert left the family business to set up on his own, Rankin and Tom decided to collaborate on the construction of caravans. Tom would build the caravans and Rankin would sell them.

A 10ft Mobile Home caravan made by Tom Propert & Son for Caravan Park towed by a 1923 Fiat 510 Sports re-styled by Tom Propert (Australia, c1939)

Several caravans were conceived and developed by Tom Propert and Rankin under the Covered Wagon and Mobile Home brand names in about 1936 and 1937. In November 1937 a company called Caravan Park was formed by Rankin to sell and hire these caravans. The caravans were manufactured in a range of sizes by Tom Propert alongside his traditional motor body building business. Tom's larger caravans were predominantly of composite construction with wooden frames, steel sides and canvas roofs. Caravan Park began trading at Tom's premises but in 1938 established its own sales premises across the road. Rankin established a caravan hire business in the same year.

A rare 1938 Caravan Park sales brochure (probably its first) indicates that the company was not only selling a range of locally built, oval-shaped Mobile Home caravans but also testing local demand for US-style travel trailers. The name of the company suggests that Rankin wanted to sell a broad range of caravans. It appears though that Australian appetite for US-style RV products was limited, since none seem to have been built or sold by Caravan Park. Tom meanwhile produced caravans not just for Rankin. He is likely to have been the builder of a commercial demonstration caravan for the Blue Ray Gas Company in 1937 and may have built leisure caravans for other private clients.

Meanwhile, Alf Propert had come up with a few RV ideas of his own. Alf's first idea was a basic caravan designed for use by road surveyors and bridge builders called The Cabin Coach. His more advanced RV concept was a US-style caravan called The Open Road which was built in De Luxe and Junior forms from about 1938. Although similar in shape to steel-built US travel trailers, it was made of lighter aluminium.

The pre-war RV products of both Alf Propert and Caravan Park are neatly captured in a series of 1939 photos of a National Roads and Motorists' Association (NRMA) caravan exhibition in Sydney (overleaf). On one side of an aisle is a large Caravan Park display prominently featuring Rankin's name along with several Mobile Home caravans and a small goods trailer made by Tom Propert called the Little Giant. On the other side of the aisle is Alf's US-style, aluminium Open Road caravan.

After the Second World War, Alf returned to building motor bodies until his death in 1949, whilst Tom's son, Tom Junior, became the man behind the Propert Patent Folding Caravan in 1952. Rankin focused on his caravan hire business during the war, hiring out caravans of various makes to displaced or homeless families. After the war Rankin established Caravan Park's own manufacturing facility in Newcastle in 1946, launching two new caravans, the Superb and the Hunter. The Superb was steel-clad and may have been based on a pre-war prototype built by Tom Propert. Caravan Park was renamed Carapark in 1950.

As roads improved and tow vehicles became more powerful in the late 1930s, the flexibility and value for money offered by large, fully-featured and sometimes heavy caravans became irresistible to many Australians. The first dedicated caravan parks started appearing in the mid-1930s and significantly enhanced the popularity of the hobby. State-based and manufacturer-sponsored caravan clubs and associations were formed to promote caravanning and advertise suitable destinations to take a caravan. The Australian love affair with the caravan had begun.

The interior of a Caravan Park Mobile Home caravan (Australia, 1939)

The National Roads and Motorists' Association ('NRMA') caravan exhibition in Sydney, with the Caravan Park display on the right and Alf Propert's Open Road US-style coach trailer at bottom left (Australia, 1939)

Australian Motorhomes of the 1930s

The motorhome, whilst playing a poor second fiddle to the caravan during the 1930s, did not expire completely. One pragmatic solution to the high cost of coach-built motorhomes was to mount a finished caravan onto a truck chassis. Oldsmobile dealers Moran Motors of Brisbane delivered one such hybrid RV to a resident in Sandgate in 1936. It had three bunks, a wardrobe, a sink and two dressing rooms. Winchester of the UK had tried out a similar combination, but on appearance grounds alone the marriage of caravan and truck proved to be a less than happy one.

A more refined if far costlier solution was to create a motorhome from a Rolls-Royce. South Melbourne-based company Romany Road Caravans built both caravans and motorhomes during the mid to late 1930s. Whilst Romany Road built motorhomes to order on Ford V8 chassis, their most prestigious product was a unique motorhome built in 1938 on a Rolls-Royce 40/50hp chassis for industrial magnate G.R. Nicholas of Melbourne.

Romany Road's other claim to fame was to provide a support caravan for cyclist Sir Hubert 'Oppy' Opperman's record-breaking run from Perth to Sydney in 1937. The benefits of any publicity arising from these ventures were however short lived – Romany Road Caravans went into liquidation in 1940.

During the 1930s self-built motorhomes continued to be built, but rarely reached the quality of the one designed by Australia's most prolific motoring explorer, Francis Birtles.

A 'streamlined' caravan on an Oldsmobile chassis in Sandgate, Brisbane (Australia, 1936)

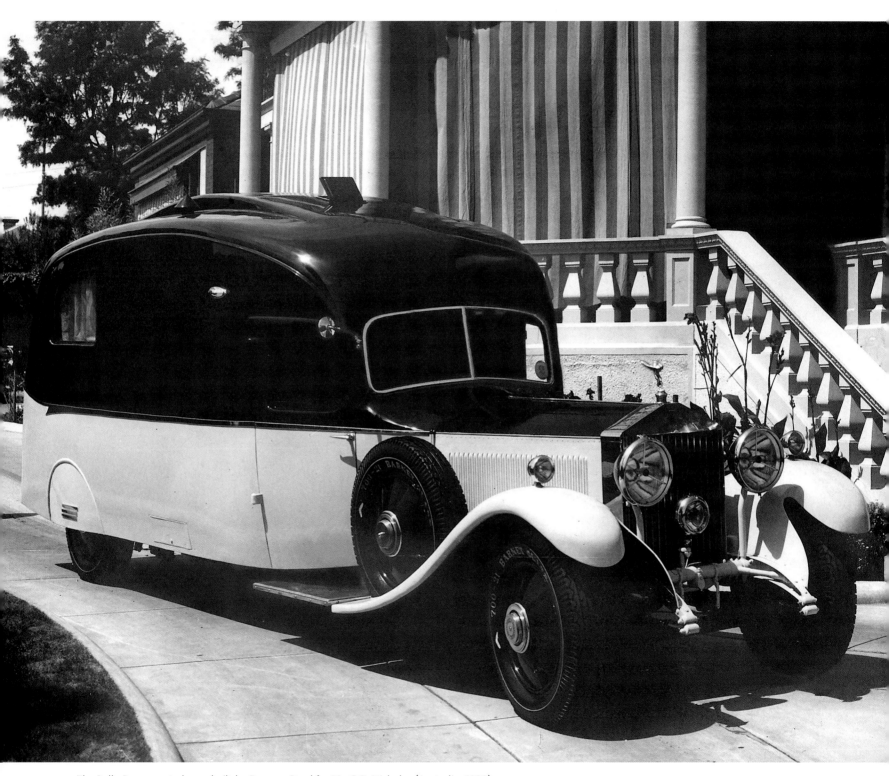

The Rolls-Royce motorhome built by Romany Road for Mr. G.R. Nicholas (Australia, 1938)

Francis Birtles and his wife Nea with mascot in front of their Ford motorhome (Australia, 1935)

Between 1908 and 1928 Birtles crossed Australia on a bicycle several times, drove from Perth to Sydney in twenty-eight days, drove a Ford Model T from Queensland to Victoria and later around Australia, explored the Australian outback, conducted road and air surveys for new railways and set several speed or non-stop records driving between Sydney, Melbourne, Adelaide, Perth and Darwin. Perhaps his best-known motoring achievement is a nine-month journey in 1927-8 from London to Melbourne in a Bean motor car nicknamed 'Sundowner'. During these adventures he found sponsors, wrote articles and books, took photos and made movies. He also had many encounters with Indigenous Australians and found gold in Arnhem Land, leaving him a wealthy man.

Birtles' 1935 Ford V8 motorhome offered a more sedate way of travelling around the country. Designed by Birtles himself, it included an insulated ceiling, 80-gallon water tanks, mosquito-proof windows, electric radiator, radio, collapsible tables and a latex rubber mattress. Most importantly, it also included 'a specially prepared line for catching crocodiles'. Because of his fame, Birtles' travels were reported wherever he went. This publicity would have been certain to present the joys of owning a motorhome to still unconvinced Australians.

Whilst the Australian RV industry before 1939 was small by comparison to the USA or the UK, the country had belatedly but assuredly developed an RV style all of its own. By the start of the Second World War, despite the notable efforts of Birtles, Romany Road and a few other motorhome builders, the flexibility and value for money offered by the caravan made it Australia's favourite form of RV. But the Australian caravan had to have good ventilation, good ground clearance, adequate streamlining and plenty of water, features which are still common today. The Australian caravan of the twenty-first century is in fact so feature-loaded that the industry is now suffering from something of an obesity epidemic. Whilst the caravan remains the dominant form of RV, a reminder of the industry's simpler, lighter days should not therefore come amiss.

CHAPTER 7

NEW ZEALAND

"

It is a rich life – rich with fragrant memories, rich with splendid scenes, rich with pleasurable moments and days, rich with healthful growth, rich with quiet intellectual peace and expansion. In short, the real simple life de luxe is undoubtedly the life of the caravan.

"

A. J. Heighway, from the *Otago Witness*, 27 December 1911

The motor caravan of William Reynolds touring the South Island (New Zealand, 1935)

New Zealand was an early adopter of the RV. New Zealanders have always been receptive to new ideas from overseas and were quick not only to spot the leisure potential of this new hobby, but also to adapt vehicles to local conditions. International tourism also stimulated growth of the industry. Despite its geographical remoteness from Europe and America, New Zealand has welcomed international tourists since Victorian times. The opening of the Suez Canal in 1869 shortened steamship journey times to Asia and Oceania considerably, allowing more international tourists to explore New Zealand's mountains, forests, lakes, rivers and geysers for the first time. One or two wealthy tourists brought horse-drawn wagons with them to tour New Zealand or had a wagon made locally. Prominent among these were hunters and fishermen, attracted to the country by reports of its unspoiled landscapes and natural bounty.

Permanent settlers in New Zealand played an important role in the establishment of a local RV industry. Some early British settlers would have seen horse-drawn circus and gypsy wagons in use in their home country and sought to replicate them for personal or business use. Farmers migrating from Europe to New Zealand in the late nineteenth century will have been familiar with shepherd's huts and living vans and brought these ideas with them. A few of these were converted to mobile recreational use or became the forerunners of the iconic New Zealand holiday home known as the bach. At the end of the nineteenth century stories of the exploits of Dr Gordon Stables and the gentlemen gypsies of the UK reached New Zealand, prompting a few more adventurous New Zealanders to explore the country in a horse-drawn wagon.

(from left to right) Janet, Minnie, Alice and Sue Dickson camping with their wagon and tent at the Pareora River near Timaru. Two boys slept in the tent. The wagon may have been built by their father William Dickson who reportedly ran a night cart business. Extra canvas was used on the wagon roof, possibly to reduce leaks or retain heat (New Zealand, c1905-1910)

1880-1910

One of the earliest newspaper reports of the use of horse-drawn accommodation on wheels in New Zealand was in agriculture. On 19 June 1880, the New Zealand correspondent of the *Sydney Town and Country Journal* described a visit to Longbeach Station, a large farm about 60 miles from Christchurch owned by John Grigg. At this farm:

'The men in charge are camped in houses on wheels, reminding one, though on a much larger scale, of the gipsy vans one recollects in the old country. These are travelled from paddock to paddock, provisions, horse feed etc. being sent out to the workmen from the head station as occasion may require.'

During the 1880s a number of newspaper advertisements selling former living vans used by road contractors or farm workers proposed that they might be suitable for camping purposes. Another early form of mobile accommodation was the so-called 'bible van'. These were caravans used for preaching in remote areas and began to appear in New Zealand in the early 1880s. Special mention must go to George Brown of Auckland for his wonderfully-named *Conditional Immortality Caravan*. It was built in 1882 by local coachbuilders Cousins and Atkin and contained two bunks, recesses for religious tracts and a platform from which the lecturer could hold forth. Further examples of bible vans are included in Chapter Eight.

The first record of a horse-drawn vehicle purpose-built for leisure in New Zealand appears in 1889, only four years after Dr Gordon Stables' *Wanderer*. Made by Rangiora coachbuilders Reeves and Son for G. Palmer-Chapman, a former planter from Cust in North Canterbury, it was made to a design submitted by Palmer-Chapman for 'travelling and camping in'. The caravan was a modest 6ft wide by 6ft long and 6ft high, with two couches used for sleeping, a door on each side and two round windows at the rear for observation purposes. There was provision for a groom to sleep in a bunk at the front and seating for between eight to ten people on the roof. It was to be pulled by between two and four horses.

The design seems to have had its shortcomings, however. On the caravan's first outing towards Nelson and the West Coast, due to its 'top heaviness' the caravan couldn't be stopped for over a mile on a downhill road into Waikari, causing damage to its springs. Then, near the Hanmer Plains Hot Springs, the caravan overturned completely in a riverbed. A five-shilling reward offered by Palmer-Chapman for a 'long straight brass coach-horn' lost on the journey gives some

indication of the damage the caravan must have suffered. Although the caravan had to be returned to Rangiora by train and the coachbuilder went bankrupt shortly after, Palmer-Chapman had the caravan repaired and continued to use it until his death in 1892.

Hunting and fishing play an important role in the development of early recreational caravanning in New Zealand. In 1892 a fisherman by the name of Hayhurst erected a 'commodious house on wheels' at Rangitata, 'so that camping is robbed of its inconveniences'. In 1900 a Mr Clark of Waimate owned 'a capital travelling house on wheels, fitted with bunks, cooking stove and every convenience' for use on his fishing excursions.

Later, in 1904, we see the first grainy image of a recreational caravan built for fisherman and deer hunter Gordon Shaw, a regular visitor to New Zealand from Western Australia. Made by coachbuilders Hordern & White of Dunedin, it measured 8ft long by 5ft 3in wide by 6ft high. It weighed 13cwt and was designed to be drawn by two horses on steep roads and one horse on level ground. Unlike the earlier caravan of Palmer-Chapman it had a powerful brake and strong undercarriage for use on the roughest roads.

The most interesting design feature of these early horse-drawn recreational vehicles is that they are short and tall. Although this may have presented some early stability problems, it seems that the narrow and winding roads of New Zealand played a part in RV design, keeping them short

A caravan constructed by Hordern & White coachbuilders of Dunedin for Gordon Shaw (New Zealand, 1904)

enough to navigate sharp bends but still tall enough to stand up in. This feature persisted all the way through to the motor-drawn caravans of the 1930s.

In 1907 we start to see the impact of motorized transport on camping in New Zealand and to get an early insight into why motorhomes, or motor caravans as they are called in New Zealand, became so popular. That year, English tourists Captain Hope-Johnstone and Mr Earle, keen hunters and fishermen, decided to have a horse-drawn caravan built by the same coachbuilders (Cousins and Atkin of Auckland) who made Brown's *Conditional Immortality Caravan* of 1882. Their caravan was equipped with lantern windows, lockers, gun and fishing racks and two tents to be fixed to the sides. It was internally lined with New Zealand timbers and had plush cushions and furnishings. The vehicle would have made quite a spectacle outside the Grand Hotel in Auckland on New Year's Day 1908 as the two tourists departed south.

Two months into their journey from Auckland to Wellington, Hope-Johnstone and Earle abandoned the horse-drawn caravan for a '43 horse-power automobile' at Rotorua. Earle later explained why:

'Owing to the lateness of the season, as also the glorious uncertainty of the weather, touring in a caravan is not what it may appear to be to those who have not had the personal experience. The condition of the roads in the majority of the parts of the Dominion is too appalling to describe.'

A recurring theme of RV travel accounts in New Zealand from the late 1890s until the early 1930s is poor road quality, often caused by flood damage. From an early date, motorhomes or 'motor caravans' became preferable to 'trailer caravans' in New Zealand because they were perceived to be able to overcome these conditions more easily than a trailer under tow.

1910-1939

Prior to the First World War, the 'picnic habit' as it was known in New Zealand began to be practised by city residents venturing out for the day or perhaps a weekend to a local beach or river. Organised tours for fishing, sightseeing and health-seeking purposes were arranged by local transport companies using a horse-drawn caravan, tents and riding horses. Caravan holidays were particularly popular in the Canterbury district of the South Island due to better, flatter roads, although the South Island's west coast was still challenging to reach. In 1911 one walker who hiked between Dunedin and Christchurch met

five caravans in four nights and determined that caravans had consequently become very popular.

During the First World War, pleasure pursuits diminished as New Zealand became involved in a conflict half a world away. Either side of the war the potential of vehicles containing accommodation, both motorized and horse-drawn, were explored for a broad range of uses in New Zealand including soil sampling (1911), post-war fund raising (1919) and a health van which toured Maori settlements in the Bay of Islands (1919).

After the war, horse-drawn caravans were gradually being replaced by the automobile for health-restoring pleasure trips. Those still selling horse-drawn caravans had to appeal to a broad audience – one advertised for sale in 1919 was marketed as being suitable for 'campers, contractors or rabbiters'. But campers now had other options.

Between 1920 and 1930, leisure travellers moved firmly away from horse-drawn caravans, first to 'auto camping' and then to motorhomes. Tents would accompany automobiles and be erected alongside them. One reporter commented that 'it was not an uncommon sight in the country districts to see a motor-car drawn up alongside the road in the evening of a summer night with a tent close by and a happy party enjoying a meal'.

But before long, 'auto camping' was to be replaced by the motorhome and the trailer caravan. There were two key developments that increased the acceptance of motorhomes and caravans in New Zealand in the 1920s – better roads and the introduction of 'motor camps'. Rugged terrain and frequent road flooding after heavy rains made long-distance road travel unreliable and sometimes dangerous. But a concerted effort

Early horse-drawn wagons were often used to carry tents and other camping equipment rather than serve as accommodation (New Zealand, 1919)

The first motor-drawn caravans in New Zealand were home built, such as this one from the 1920s (New Zealand, c1920s)

to improve road conditions in the 1920s and 1930s enhanced year-round accessibility and safety. Once tourists felt it was safe to travel by automobile for camping and leisure, a number of local councils and automobile associations established 'motor camps' near the main tourist attractions, providing key services including water, camp kitchens and basic amenities. Although many preferred to 'free camp' outside of these camps (and still do today), the provision of motor camps brought greater comforts to early RV owners and increased tourism in those regions which established them.

The idea of taking a holiday in a motorhome started to crystallise in New Zealand in the early 1920s. Auckland Ford dealers John W. Andrew and Son advertised in a local newspaper in 1923 that they were 'open to supply "Ford" Caravan on Truck Chassis, equipped with bunks, stove, electric light and all conveniences for touring New Zealand'. In 1924 local papers reported that 'a motor lorry with a fair-sized tent erected upon it' passed through Timaru, while in the same

year a motorhome 'fitted up in a most convenient style' was displayed at the Agricultural and Pastoral Show in Stratford. A few entrepreneurial motorhome owners carried advertising on their sides from local businesses, generating income from the adverts to help cover holiday costs.

One of the earliest photos of a New Zealand motorhome is that belonging to W.H. Gibson, a novelty jeweller from Auckland known locally as 'The Gold Wire King'. Based on a Dodge Brothers chassis, it weighed 15cwt and afforded 'ample and comfortable accommodation for two persons'. Its rather austere interior indicates it was a basic conversion of a commercial truck body, and with Gibson's business address inscribed on the side of the van, it may even have been a converted delivery van.

An important figure in the early days of New Zealand's motorized RV history was motor body builder H. Parker of Dunedin. In 1926 Parker developed Parker's Extending Motor Caravan, a 12ft motorhome built on a 1-ton Ford

Above: Early motor caravans were sparsely fitted out trucks or delivery vans, such as this Dodge Brothers motor caravan constructed in Auckland for W.H. Gibson (New Zealand, 1924)

Right: An advert for Dunedin-based Parkerbilt Folding Trailer Caravans (New Zealand, 1934)

chassis that was extendable at the rear to 19ft. Described in company advertising as a 'safe, comfortable and movable crib on wheels', the vehicle's party piece was a rear wall that dropped down to become a floor which was then covered by a sliding canvas frame. In 1931 Parker moved into the camper trailer market, patenting a collapsible trailer called the Parkerbilt Folding Trailer Caravan. When folded down it was only 3ft 6in high, increasing to 7ft 10in when fully raised. It weighed only 6cwt and could therefore be towed by low-powered automobiles. Parker's camper trailer was probably the first to be locally built in New Zealand. Parker sold these trailers until about 1936.

Camper trailers were popular with hardy campers but less so with the 'picnickers'. Casual campers enjoyed the flexibility of a trailer but needed more protection from New Zealand's variable weather. The popularity in the UK of solid-walled, full height caravans towed by automobiles was noted in the New Zealand press from the early 1920s onwards. The first locally-built motor-drawn caravans were self-built and began to appear in the mid-1920s. Gradual improvements in road conditions helped to make trailer towing easier, albeit initially by a brave few. In 1925 a Mr W. King from Christchurch built his own caravan using a motor axle and suspension. Its walls were made of three-ply timber

WEEKENDS..
..ANYWHERE

FOLDED READY FOR THE ROAD..
.. IN 30 SECONDS!

PARKERBILT FOLDER TRAILER CARAVANS.
Made entirely in N.Z. by H. PARKER, Motor Body Builder, Anderson's Bay Road, Dunedin.

and its roof of sheet iron. The interior was 'tastefully finished in purple and gold' and the ceiling was made of white calico. Weighing a not insignificant 10cwt, the estimated cost of the caravan was £80. In 1929 a Mr S. Freeman from Palmerston North built a somewhat lighter caravan made from Masonite – it weighed only 7cwt.

Probably the first New Zealand caravan to be manufactured commercially in limited numbers was the Davey Trailer Caravan, made by Charles Davey of Auckland in 1931. Launched at the Auckland Winter Exhibition of July 1931, the Davey Trailer Caravan adopted the short, tall form of New Zealand's early horse-drawn caravans. The caravans could be built to order from £85 or hired from £4 per week. For reasons unknown the company had only a short life until the end of 1931 when the business was put up for sale.

A number of motor body works companies made small quantities of caravans for sale or hire, particularly in the latter half of the 1930s. The self-built caravan was also popular. During the 1930s a few UK caravans including Eccles, Winchesters and Car Cruisers were personally imported into New Zealand by migrants or long-term tourists. Rice camper trailers were also imported by at least one commercial dealer.

The Bunnythorpe Garage in Palmerston North was one example of a motor body workshop building caravans to its own design. Its proprietor L. Weston-Webb built caravans in at least two different sizes for his clients.

There's a thrill in...

CARAVANING

With a caravan attached to your car you have the freedom of the country. Choose the by-paths and leafy tracks, stop where you wish, eliminate hotel expenses and the worries of a formal life. You can rest while you're caravaning.

Tour with Economy in a

Davey Trailer Caravan

For Hire at very reasonable charges—See them at the Show

When you see one of these Caravans you'll soon imagine all the delights it can bring you. There's a new thrill and romance brought to your holidays. You're relieved from all thought of time—and the cost is comparatively low. Get price particulars at Stall No. 41 at the Winter Exhibition.

CHARLES DAVEY, BOX 833, AUCKLAND.

Above: An advert for Auckland-based Davey Trailer Caravans (New Zealand, 1931)

Below: A caravan imported from the UK, probably an Eccles collapsible caravan, on the streets of Auckland (New Zealand, 1930s)

As caravan popularity increased, local garages such as the Bunnythorpe Garage in Palmerston North made caravans to their own design (New Zealand, 1935)

A lightly-fenestrated caravan constructed by L. Weston-Webb of the Bunnythorpe Garage in Palmerston North (New Zealand, 1935)

Perhaps the best-known New Zealand caravan manufacturer of the 1930s was Auckland-based Tanner Trailers. In 1936 the company first appeared as a vendor of the Parkerbilt Special Caravan, but in November 1936 Tanners started advertising for sale or hire its own 13ft Tourist 4-berth Special, an oval-shaped, full-height caravan. By 1937 Tanner Trailers were building a range of six oval-shaped caravans from a 9ft model designed for 7hp automobiles to a deluxe 15ft model for 16hp automobiles. Late in 1937 a US-style travel trailer was also advertised. Tanners continued to build caravans or caravan chassis into the 1950s.

The Caravan Company, later shortened to Caravanco, was another Auckland-based caravan manufacturer of the late 1930s. Its marketing catchphrase was a tongue-twisting 'caravans conscientiously constructed'. Its products first appeared in 1938 and by 1939 it was building for sale and hire a range of six caravans in the 10-12ft range. Lantern roofs were incorporated into some of their models.

At the start of 1939, an interesting collaboration commenced between Christchurch engineer J.E. Moore and Schult Trailers of the USA (see pages 138-139), whereby caravans were produced in New Zealand by Moore under licence from Schult at a Christchurch factory. In 1939 alone Moore-Schult Trailers produced over 100 caravans, including both large US-style trailers

A deluxe 2-berth Tanner caravan suitable for 10hp cars (New Zealand, 1937)

and small, oval trailers better suited to New Zealand roads and small automobiles. Production continued until late 1940.

Other small-scale commercial caravan builders of the 1930s included Andersons Motor Body Works (Dunedin, 1931-35), The New Zealand Trailer and Caravan Company (Auckland, 1936-37), H.V. Hayman's Stowaway Caravan Trailer (Birkenhead, 1936-38) and Runlite (Dunedin, 1939). An example of the ingenious Stowaway Caravan Trailer is included in the collection of the Museum of Transport and Technology ('MOTAT') in Auckland.

Caravan clubs played an important role in popularising the RV lifestyle. The first New Zealand caravan club was formed in 1933 in Cambridge, with most early members owning self-built caravans. The Auckland Caravan Club was formed later in the decade and exchanged regular visits with the Cambridge Club. The Automobile Association of Canterbury formed a caravan section in 1938 to ensure the growth of the activity was not unduly restricted by government regulation.

As in a number of other countries, the 1930s in New Zealand was the decade of the caravan. By 1939 it was estimated that there were more than 9,000 caravan registrations in New Zealand, with Christchurch and Auckland having the largest number. But unlike some other countries, New Zealand did not fall out of love with the motorhome, which maintained its popularity alongside the caravan throughout the 1930s. There was a general perception that a motorhome was better at navigating New Zealand's poor and narrow roads, especially if a driver had to reverse due to an oncoming flock of sheep.

At the start of the 1930s it was estimated by one newspaper that there were only fifty recreational motorhomes in New Zealand. Although exact numbers are not known, this number grew significantly during the decade. Many were self-built or custom-made by local garages or body builders, with conversions from public buses being especially popular.

By the start of the Second World War, both motorhomes and caravans had become common sights on New Zealand's roads. The RV holiday had evolved into one of the most popular recreational activities in the nation for 'Kiwis' and visitors alike. Today, the RV is an important part of New Zealand's leisure culture. In recognition of their significance, a 1937 self-built caravan forms part of the collection of the Museum of New Zealand, Te Papa Tongarewa, in Wellington.

A 10ft 4-berth Moore-Schult caravan built in New Zealand under licence from Schult Trailers of the USA (New Zealand, 1939)

An automobile and caravan, possibly a Moore-Schult, in front of Central Motors Garage in Nelson (New Zealand, 1939)

Above: A meeting of the Cambridge Caravan Club in 1936. Many club members built their own caravans (New Zealand, 1936)

Below: The converted motor bus of the Davidson family (New Zealand, 1934)

CHAPTER 8

SPECIAL PURPOSE COACHES, CARAVANS AND MOTORHOMES

The caravan will be of great importance in the automobile world of tomorrow. The traveller will tow one behind his car to carry any amount of baggage, tools and spares. The grand tourist will turn it into his home on wheels. The doctor who has to travel will tow a caravan, well appointed with equipment and instruments to carry out his difficult art. We will see the X-ray caravan, the small mobile surgery, the sterile room for urgent operations in the field of battle. The small industrialist, the businessman and the modern travelling salesman will each have a caravan specialized for their trade.

Baudry de Saunier (France, 1919)

As manufacturers around the world responded to the wishes of their customers by building vehicles designed for recreation, other uses for these mobile and flexible creations became apparent. Consequently, not all early caravans and motorhomes were used for leisure. Frenchman Baudry de Saunier was one of the first to recognize the potential of the caravan for a wide range of applications beyond tourism. Every one of the predictions he made in 1919 about the future of the caravan has come to pass.

Diversification of caravans and motorhomes beyond recreational use was not accidental. The construction of special purpose vehicles helped a number of RV manufacturers stay afloat during times of recession and war, or simply provided extra income until RVs became mainstream. The specialized requirements of vehicles built for businesspeople, politicians and missionaries would sometimes lead to new features that would be fed back into RVs. The mobility, space and accommodation options offered by caravans and motorhomes was a boon to those who needed to spread their message remotely or sell their products or services to those who could not or would not travel. Flexibility in design was the key, and as this chapter will show, creativity was essential.

An RV on Rails – The Camp Coach

The Depression of the early 1930s caused significant hardship in many parts of the UK. Those who had jobs were forced to work long hours with perhaps only the occasional day's holiday during the year. As economic conditions improved, so did the demands from workers for more time off. The Holidays with Pay Act was eventually introduced in 1938, giving paid holidays to workers for the first time. Holiday camps such as Butlins (the first was built in 1936) and caravan parks met with strong demand.

One unusual and mildly eccentric form of 'recreational vehicle' that met with some success in the UK during the 1930s was the railway 'camp coach'. These were retired railway coaches placed in sidings at holiday destination railway stations and rented out to holidaymakers.

Trialled successfully in 1933 by the London & North Eastern Railway, other railway companies soon followed with more coaches in their regions, including the Great Western Railway ('GWR'). The camp coach opposite was operated by the GWR in 1934 at a siding at Gara Bridge in Devon. Coaches were adapted to include kitchens, beds and bathrooms and were rented out at about £3 per week. Posters advertising these unusual railway holidays could be found at stations across the network. The concept was suspended during wartime but revitalized after the war by the newly nationalized British Railways in 1948.

Religion

Horse-drawn 'bible carts' were used by missionaries and people of faith in rural areas around the world during the second half of the nineteenth century and beyond. Because these vehicles often travelled long distances, they invariably included sleeping facilities. Their later motorized derivatives, variously called bible vans, gospel cars, missionary vans and mobile chapels, became fairly sophisticated from the 1920s onwards, incorporating speaking platforms and even organs. Where there was insufficient space for permanent beds, it was not unknown for travelling pastors to sleep on small pews inside their mobile churches.

The three examples shown here demonstrate the ingenuity of ministers across the ages who had vehicles built that would attract maximum attention. The *Binskins Itinerant Bible Carriage* (below) is from Oamaru in New Zealand in about 1910. The *Gospel Car No. 1* (opposite top) belonged to 'Wm Downer' of the USA but is of unknown date. The *Gospel Ark Trailer* (opposite bottom) is from the USA in 1937 and features a mobile chapel design that may have reflected contemporary interest in airships.

War

'A caravan forms a safe, comfortable and economical retreat during wartime' claimed a London caravan sales company advert in 1939, perhaps with just a hint of quiet desperation. But in fact caravans did become a common place of escape from cities affected by war. They also served a wide range of other wartime uses.

Towards the end of the First World War, British Caravan Club Secretary J. Harris Stone received a request from General Haig for as many caravans as the club could muster to be sent abroad to help the war effort. They were to be used for war planning, map reading and the use of nurses. Harris Stone later reported that he 'worked night and day and telegraphed all over the country and was able to dispatch a large number to the front in the required time'. Most of these caravans never returned to the UK.

The photograph opposite shows how some British recreational caravans were used during the Battle of the Somme between July and November 1916. They were used as refreshment caravans for the 'walking wounded'. This image appeared much later in an advert for Winchester caravans in October 1939 stating that they had been manufactured by Bertram Hutchings for wartime use.

In the First World War, Hutchings of Winchester Caravans was also commissioned by the UK Royal Navy to build a mobile war recruiting office (below). Caravans and motorhomes closer to the battlefields played an important role as the war progressed as map reading rooms, mobile hospitals, radio vans and military accommodation.

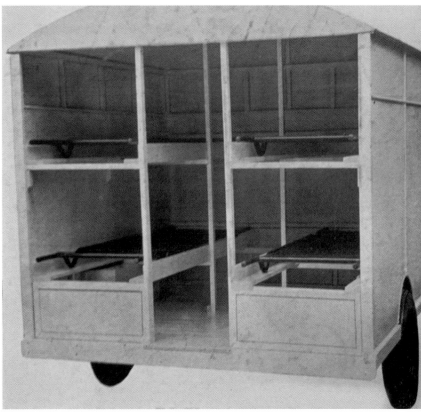

In the Second World War, touring caravans were used by the Red Cross for wartime administration (above left). Raven Caravans were one of a number of manufacturers who converted their recreational caravans into ambulances (above right), an ironic twist given that the design of some early British caravans had been influenced by the ambulance trailers of the First World War. Caravans were used informally as temporary housing in the UK for some of the 1.5 million evacuees removed from cities as part of Operation Pied Piper in 1939. They later served as shelters for those made homeless by wartime bombing. Some (right) were crudely camouflaged, although this precaution would prove to be of limited benefit. According to caravan historian W.M. Whiteman, recreational caravans were not intended for long term occupation and suffered badly from poor insulation that led to mould, dampness and even fires from temporary stoves installed by occupants to keep warm. One side-effect of living in a caravan in wartime was the benefit of its suspension, which according to a number of reports helped the vehicle to absorb the shockwaves from an air raid more effectively than a fixed structure. This effect was, according to Whiteman, also noticed by the USA when the US government used caravans as support vehicles during the nuclear tests of the 1950s.

Women's Suffrage

The growth in leisure caravanning in the early 1900s coincided with the rise of the Suffrage movement in the UK. According to Angela Willis, curator of the UK's Caravan and Motorhome Club archives, 'horse-drawn caravans were used by several Suffrage organisations to spread the message on voting rights for women amongst rural communities. Rallies were held wherever the caravans went, occasionally leading to spirited exchanges with the locals about whether women should be permitted to vote. About one third of Caravan Club members were women, including some Suffragettes who used militant forms of protest. Women did not receive full voting rights in Britain until 1928.'

The image on the previous page from 1908 shows a Suffrage caravan being used to address a public gathering at Whitby Harbour, Yorkshire. The image below is also from 1908 and shows some members of the Suffrage movement in front of their caravan. Charlotte Despard, founder of the Women's Freedom League, is to the left of the window.

Politics

Caravans were used to help convey political messages to people in remote areas well before the Suffragette movement. The English Land Restoration League operated five caravans to promote land tax reform from 1891. Five years later, socialism was the key message of the so-called 'Clarion Vans'. Named after the weekly socialist newspaper *The Clarion* and designed to offer a platform for women to express their political views in public, Clarion Vans were pioneered by women's columnist Julia Dawson in 1896. These vans visited towns and villages in England and Scotland until 1929, and were used to hold Socialist Party open air meetings and sell socialist literature. The van in the photograph (right) is an early Clarion Van from around 1900. It served as a soup van offering bowls of broth for a farthing to the poor and unemployed of Liverpool during winter.

Caravans continued to be used for political purposes in a number of western democracies throughout the first half of the twentieth century. In the USA, the Democratic National Committee used a small fleet of trailers (below) to help re-elect President Franklin D. Roosevelt in the US presidential elections of 1936. Each trailer was equipped with a loudspeaker and a speaking platform. The trailers must have helped to get the job done - President Roosevelt won the election in a sweeping victory over Governor Alf Landon.

Health

Caravans and motorhomes have a long history of providing health services and health education to remote communities or during outbreaks of disease.

One example is the use of horse-drawn caravans to provide basic medical assistance to French citizens during the First World War. The caravan in the photograph below was a mobile dental clinic. This caravan is marked as providing support for a 'depôt d'éclopés', which was a medical facility for treating the war wounded before being sent back to the front. This image shows predominantly women receiving dental treatment in a city street.

After the First World War, community health became an important issue in a number of countries. Dr Marie Stopes, for example, was a pioneer in birth control. Dr Stopes established the UK's first static family planning centre in London in 1921. With strong views on the need for better family planning education amongst the poor, in about 1920 she adapted a horse-drawn caravan (opposite top) and took it into the communities she was trying to reach. The letters 'CBC' on the caravan probably stand

for her birth control philosophy of the time, 'Constructive Birth Control'. Her endeavours proved successful and she gradually built up a small network of clinics across the UK. Marie Stopes International now works in thirty-seven countries around the world 'to help women and girls to have children by choice, not chance'.

In 1937 the adaptability of the Curtiss Aerocar was demonstrated. That year the US Public Health Service commissioned a specially fitted out Aerocar (right) to assist in the war against syphilis. A complete trailer laboratory, the vehicle was used in Georgia, USA to help detect and treat a disease which would affect hundreds of thousands of people until the arrival of penicillin in the 1940s.

Education

As long as families have lived in movable homes, attempts have been made to provide education for itinerant children. In the early twentieth century, offers by British local councils to incorporate the children of mobile communities into permanent schools were often half-hearted, since in the eyes of local communities such offers could lead to itinerants overstaying their welcome. So gypsies, circus and fairground families have all sought to educate children in their own mobile classrooms. The classroom in the photograph below formed part of a permanent fairground in Paris. The photograph was taken in 1919 at France's oldest funfair, *La Foire du Trône*.

Another important educational tool which benefitted from early caravan and motorhome design was the mobile library or 'bookmobile'. Mobile libraries have a long history. One of the earliest know is from the UK, the Warrington Mechanics Institution Perambulating Library of 1860. Vehicles that were designed for short distance use were in the main converted trucks, but long-distance bookmobiles would sometimes include accommodation for the roving librarian. The photograph opposite is of a Cincinnati, Ohio bookmobile in 1927.

Food and Entertainment

The provision of food from mobile vehicles has a long tradition. The American horse-drawn 'night lunch wagon' served food and drink to city-based night shift workers from the 1880s onwards and became the forerunner of today's food trucks and hot dog stands. Some were highly elaborate. The photo opposite shows a Thornycroft steam wagon built for the Caravan Restaurant Co. Ltd in the UK in 1904. Its ownership and usage are unknown, but it would have been one of the earliest motorized food vehicles. It is the only known steam-driven food truck from the early 1900s.

In addition to manufacturing special purpose vehicles for the domestic market, UK vehicle manufacturers and coachbuilders also welcomed orders from all parts of the British Empire, however unusual. Entertainment came in many forms at that time, including shooting game. The Shooting Box (below)

was a special purpose caravan built by an unknown London manufacturer for Prince Ranjitsinhji, the Jam of Nawanagar in India, in 1907. It cost £1,000 to build and is described by the British newspaper *The Sketch* of 16 October 1907:

'[The Shooting Box] can be taken to pieces, sent by rail to a given point, and drawn from there to the jungle on a trolley by oxen or elephants. It will be left in the jungle until the animals have become accustomed to it, and then the Jam will take up his residence in the caravan, and be ready for his quarry at any time. Port-holes for the rifles are arranged at a convenient height all round the box, which has, in addition to its one main room, a bathroom and a lavatory.

'The outside of the caravan is painted a dull green, in order that it may blend with the jungle, and in the inside

also, which is decorated in the Queen Anne style, green is the prevailing colour. The sofas can be converted into beds, and there are provided writing bureaux, bridge tables, and comfortable chairs, while the floor is parquet, covered with Persian rugs. The shooting box has been made in England for the well-known firm of Leach and Weborny, of Bombay.'

The Shooting Box also had an upper deck for observing the animals. To resist the termites of the Indian jungle, the caravan had to be made from hardwood, in this case teak lined with oak. This came with a severe weight penalty – The Shooting Box weighed 10 tons. Whether the wild animals of the Indian jungle were sufficiently compliant to place themselves in front of the shooting box for immediate dispatch is not recorded.

One of the most popular forms of entertainment in the early twentieth century were the movies. The silent movies of this period were seen mainly in the cinemas of cities and large towns. For the benefit of those living further afield, so-called

'picture show men' would show movies to remote audiences. They travelled in a horse and wagon and used outdoor cloth screens or set up a screen in a tent. With the arrival of 'talkies', motorhome or trailers were later used to create so-called 'travelling cinemas'. These were used not just for entertainment purposes, but also for propaganda and political messaging.

The photo below is a postcard from 1911 showing a horse-drawn wagon in the UK promoting Australia through a series of short films under the theme of 'Wild Australia'. The photo was probably taken as part of the 1911 Festival of Empire celebrations, held initially at Crystal Palace in London followed by a national tour.

The *Touring Talkie* van (opposite top) from 1929 was a 'daylight cinema saloon' used by the Labour Party of the UK, possibly in connection with the 1929 election. The *McCall Parade* vehicle of 1935 (opposite bottom) was a US travelling cinema that brought small audiences inside the trailer to watch movies.

Business

Tailor-made commercial caravans and motorhomes were produced in many countries for individuals and corporations, ranging from the travelling salesman's showroom to a millionaire's office on wheels. Businesses appreciated the opportunity to travel to their customers, especially when times were tough and closing a sale was hard.

So-called 'brush vans' were a common sight in British towns and cities in the early twentieth century. These were travelling product showrooms used by gypsies to sell home-made wickerwork, baskets and brushes at shows and fairs and in residential areas. Usually uncomplicated affairs designed to store and display products, more elaborate brush vans were sometimes commissioned from a noted coachbuilder to attract attention. The fully-stocked brush van (opposite) from about 1900 was probably built by circus ride and living wagon builder Orton and Spooner of Burton upon Trent.

The photograph of an upholsterer's van (below) was taken in the San Francisco area of the USA in 1926. The van's design as a literal house on wheels may have drawn a crowd but would have limited the driver's vision when on the road, making it challenging to operate. Notable design features include the artificial arm hanging from the side of the house used to indicate turning direction

(operated by wire from the driver's cabin) and the wires on the roof, most likely used as a bird deterrent.

The Curtiss Aerocar was used for a wide range of activities beyond recreation including passenger bus services for hotel and rail transfers and travelling sales. The modest exterior of the 1930 Curtiss Aerocar of the Peoria Casket Company of the USA (opposite) gives little away as to its purpose, but the interior reveals a lavish display of lined caskets (coffins) for bereaved relatives to choose from.

The General Electric Refrigerator Car of 1932 (below centre) shows another commercial use from the USA of the Curtiss Aerocar. Its appearance alone would have attracted potential customers.

The Camel Pen trailer (bottom) is a classic example of an American travelling salesman's trailer from 1936. The car and trailer come from Orange, New Jersey, USA. The Camel Pen Company had a short-lived existence from 1935 to 1938. It sold pens that 'made their own ink' by adding water to ink concentrate stored inside the pen.

SELECTED WORLDWIDE RECREATIONAL VEHICLE PATENTS BEFORE 1939

Patent records offer an important design and technical resource in the study of all vehicle types, and RVs are no exception. RV designs were protected by patents to varying degrees around the world, with the USA having the largest number of RV-related patents up to the Second World War. In the late nineteenth century some makers would patent the entire RV, but as this method could be easily overcome by competitors through a change to a single component, patents later became more specific. Tow hitches, leg supports, collapsible trailers, slide-out mechanisms and even toilets were popular items to be patented. Other makers were intimidated by the potentially high cost of legally protecting a patent and simply didn't bother. Yet another group of manufacturers were happy to share ideas in the hope that the RV industry as a whole would benefit and grow. The drawings submitted with patents provide an interesting visual history of early RVs. The following diagrams are taken from RV patents from a selection of countries between 1889 and 1938.

Recreational Vehicle Patents 1889–1922

1889
McMaster Camping Vehicle (USA)

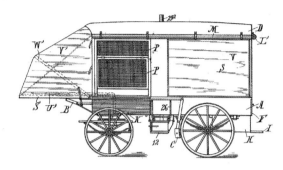

1894
Brown Hunting Wagon (USA)

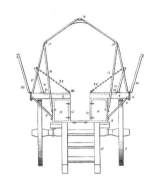

1909
Hardin Camping Wagon (USA)

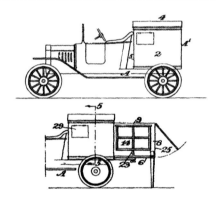

1916
De Bretteville Camping Attachment (USA)

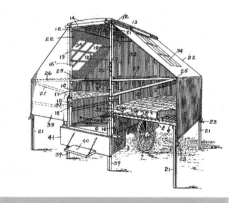

1917
Harris Trailer Camp (USA)

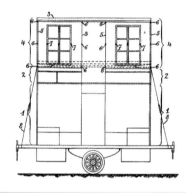

1920
Lafeuille Telescope Caravan (France)

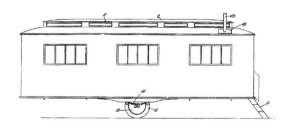

1920
Piggott Caravan (UK)

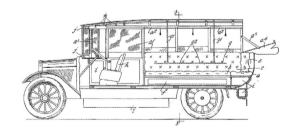

1920
Pilmore-Bedford Saloon Deluxe (UK)

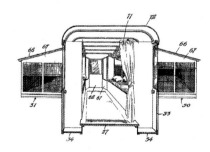

1922
Curtiss Camp Car (USA)

Recreational Vehicle Patents 1923–1933

1923
Cassell Motor Body (USA)

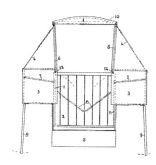

1926
Rice Folding Caravan (UK)

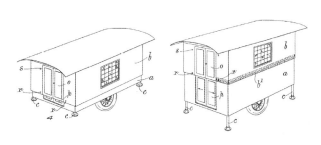

1927
Skinner Collapsible Caravan (UK)

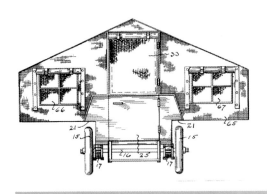

1928
Gilkison Camping Trailer (USA)

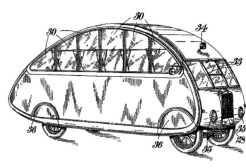

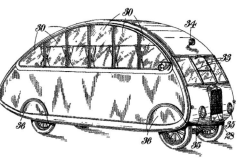

1928
Pemberton Billing Road Yacht (UK)

1929
Barber Expanding Caravan (UK)

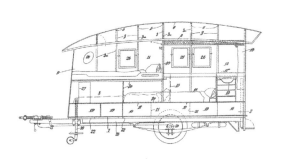

1930
Howard Mercer Caravan (UK)

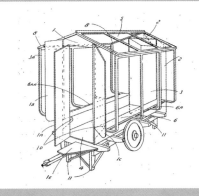

1931
Parker Camp Trailer (New Zealand)

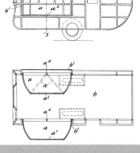

1933
Bishop Rotating Extension (UK)

Recreational Vehicle Patents 1933–1938

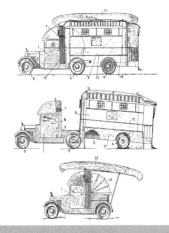

1933
Levoyer Removable Caravan (France)

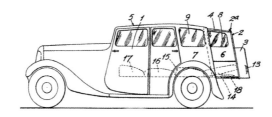

1935
Cook Extending Automobile (UK)

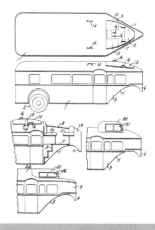

1935
Curtiss Robinson Trailer (USA)

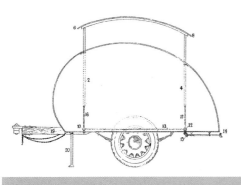

1935
Jennison Pop-Top (Australia)

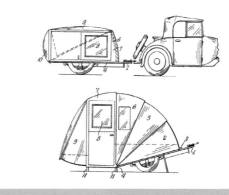

1936
Wilson Collapsible Caravan (UK)

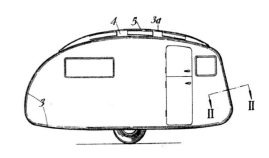

1937
Dawtrey Curved Caravan (UK)

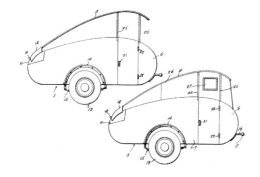

1937
Alvord Teardrop (USA)

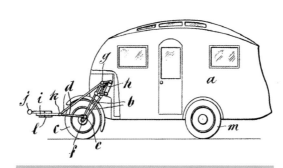

1937
Ensor Three Wheeled Caravan (UK)

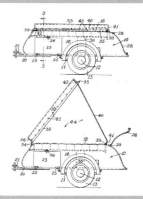

1938
Lynn A-Frame Trailer (USA)

ACKNOWLEDGEMENTS

In the UK, my profound thanks go to Angela Willis, Curator of The Caravan and Motorhome Club Collection at the National Motor Museum in Beaulieu for providing material, feedback and support throughout this project. Without Angela this book would not have been possible. I am most grateful to Peter Card and the Trustees of the Michael Sedgwick Memorial Trust for their financial support. Thanks also to John Greenwood and John Sootheran at Warners Group Publications for providing access to *The Caravan* magazine archives, Andrew Jenkinson, Kat Pearson at the Camping and Caravanning Club, the Historic Caravan Club of the UK, Richard Roberts for providing access to his wonderful collection of historic motoring newspapers and magazines, Tom Clarke for his forensic Rolls-Royce knowledge, Adrian Harvey at the Scottish Highlander Photo Archive, Malcolm Bobbitt at the Society of Automotive Historians in Britain, Dick Eastwood at The Steam Plough Club of the UK, Andy King at Bristol Culture, Neil Burdock at the Panhard et Levassor Club GB, Lin Chilcott at the Derbyshire Village Mission, the Great Western Trust and Mike Rendell.

To the supportive staff at Pen and Sword Books, especially John Scott Morgan and Janet Brookes, and to my editor Carol Trow, thank you for bringing this book to life.

In France, I am deeply grateful to French RV historians Pierre-François Dupond, Gilles Fillaud and Bruno Leroux for sharing their passion, extensive knowledge and collections of early French RV photographs. My thanks also to François Varanet, Bernard Vermeylen of Les Doyennes de Panhard et Levassor and Hervé Pannier.

In the USA, my sincere thanks to US RV historians David Woodworth and Al Hesselbart for their assistance, knowledge and photographs. A special mention goes to Joel Silvey for his profound knowledge and extensive archive of early American tent trailers. I must also express my deep gratitude to Rick Leisenring, Curator at the Glenn H. Curtiss Museum, for his patient support for this book and provision of some outstanding photographs of early Curtiss RVs. Thanks also to the RV/MH Hall of Fame in Elkhart, Terry Bone and The Tin Can Tourists, Bob Jacobsen and Roger Sherman of the Pierce-Arrow Society, Douglas Keister, Vince Martinico and Airstream Corporate Archivist Samantha Martin.

In Germany, my special thanks to Markus Böhm at the Erwin Hymer Museum for his patience and hard work in dealing with multiple research requests. Thanks also to Ulrich Kubisch, Margit Ramus, Edgar van Ommen, and Dörte, Yasmin and Uli Stelling for their kind translation assistance.

In Australia, my sincere appreciation goes to Richard Dickins, probably the most knowledgeable person in Australia on the topic of early Australian RVs. Thank you, Richard, for your research and detective work on my behalf. Thanks also go to Richard Potter, Bill Propert, Michael Tierney, Jeffry Gill, Trevor Gill, Chris Heysen, David Cook, Tori Dixon-Whittle, the Caravan and Camping Industries Association of South Australia, The Rolls-Royce Owners' Club of Australia and the members of the Vintage Caravans forum who keep the photos and memories of early Australian RVs alive. My thanks also to Collyn Rivers for his outstanding technical knowledge of towing dynamics.

In New Zealand I would like to thank the New Zealand Motor Caravan Association and its members for supplying me with some early RV photographs. My thanks also to the National Library of New Zealand for their support.

I would like to thank all the staff and supporters of libraries, archives and museums around the world who work tirelessly to make the stories and images of early RVs available to a contemporary audience. Keeping these archives open during a global pandemic allowed researchers to continue their work at a difficult time. Those deserving of a special mention are the *Gallica* archive of the Bibliothèque Nationale de France, the US Library of Congress, *Trove* of Australia and the National Library of New Zealand. Your dedicated work makes books of this kind possible.

To my parents Shirley and Don Woodmansey, thank you for introducing me to the wonderful world of caravans and for inspiring me and so many others by gathering and passing on your knowledge as parents, grandparents and teachers.

Finally, to my wife Christine and son James, thank you for supporting me in this project and all else with your positivity, patience and love.

IMAGE CREDITS

Source image reference numbers (where applicable) are shown in brackets after page reference.

Front Cover

(SFA022818480), Spaarnestad Photo

Back Cover

from the collection of Bill Propert by kind courtesy of Michael Tierney, Australia

Title Page

by the author

Preface

p7, from The Caravan and Motorhome Club Collection, UK

Introduction

p9, reproduced by permission of Airstream, Inc., USA

Chapter 1 – Recreational Vehicle Origins and Influences

p11 (RP-P-OB-84.132A), Rijksmuseum Amsterdam, Netherlands

p12 (bottom left), from *Classical Portfolio of Primitive Carriers* by M. M. Kirkman (World Railway Publishing Company, Chicago, 1895)

p12 (bottom right), from *A History of Domestic Manners and Sentiments in England During the Middle Ages* by Thomas Wright, illustration by F.W. Fairholt (Chapman and Hall, London, 1862)

p13 (LCCN 04017316), Polo, Marco, and Noah Brooks. *The story of Marco Polo*. New York, The Century co, 1899. Library of Congress, USA

p14, from *Stage-coach and Mail in Days of Yore: A Picturesque History of the Coaching Age* by C.G. Harper (Chapman and Hall, London, 1903)

p15, engraving by E. Hacker after A.E. Cooper, Wellcome Collection

p16, Mike Rendell private collection

p17 (top left) (Accession: 944-2952), 'Manders Menagerie', Tyne & Wear Archives and Museums, UK

p17 (bottom right), Bristol Culture, England

p18 (top left) (RCIN 2500439), 'Photographic Van 1855' image, Royal Collection Trust/©Her Majesty Queen Elizabeth II 2020

p18 (top right), from *Cyprus as I Saw It in 1879*, by Sir Samuel White Baker (Macmillan and Co., London, 1879)

p19, courtesy of The Steam Plough Club (UK)

p20, from *Street Life in London*, 1877, by John Thomson and Adolphe Smith, London School of Economics Library, UK

p21, © Illustrated London News Ltd/Mary Evans

p23 (Object No 85/1285-21), 'Coogee Bay, Sydney', Henry King, Sydney, Australia, c.1880-1900, Museum of Applied Arts & Sciences, Sydney, Australia

Chapter 2 – The United Kingdom

pp25, 31 (bottom left), 31 (bottom right), 34, 35, 39 (bottom), 43, 49, 50, 52 (top left), 53, 53 (inset), 61 (bottom right), 65, from The Caravan and Motorhome Club Collection, UK

p26, from *The Old Curiosity Shop* by Charles Dickens (first published in *Master Humphrey's Clock* in 1840-41)

p27 (top left), © Illustrated London News Ltd/Bridgeman

pp 27 (top right), 32, 33 (bottom left), 33 (bottom right), 47 (bottom left), 47 (bottom right), © Illustrated London News Ltd/Mary Evans

p29 (RP-F-2001-7-1096), from *The Cruise of the Land Yacht 'Wanderer'; or, Thirteen Hundred Miles in my Caravan* by Gordon Stables (Hodder and Stoughton, London, 1886), Rijksmuseum Amsterdam, Netherlands. Purchased with the support of the Mondriaan Stichting, the Prins Bernhard Cultuurfonds, the VSBfonds, the Paul Huf Fonds/Rijksmuseum Fonds and the Egbert Kunstfonds

p30 (top left), by the author, map from d-Maps.com

p30 (bottom right), from *The Cruise of the Land Yacht "Wanderer"; or, Thirteen Hundred Miles in my Caravan* by Gordon Stables (Hodder and Stoughton, London, 1886)

pp31 (top left), 42 (bottom), 44, 46, 48 (top), 48 (bottom), 51, 52 (top right), 55, 56, 58, 60, 61 (top right), 64, 66 (all), with kind permission from *The Caravan* magazine, UK

p31 (top right), Mary Evans/Grenville Collins Postcard Collection

p36 (left), 36 (right), from The Camping and Caravanning Club Archives, UK

pp37, 39, from *Caravanning and Camping-Out* by J. Harris Stone (McBride Nast & Company, New York, 1914)

p38, © The British Motor Industry Heritage Trust Film & Picture Library, UK

p39 (bottom inset), from *Motor* magazine (USA), April 1908

p41 (top), courtesy of Exeter Memories, UK

p41 (bottom), from The Martin Lumby Archive at The Historic Caravan Club, UK

p42 (top) (btv1b6926441k), from Bibliothèque nationale de France (Gallica), France

p45, from The Historic Caravan Club, UK and Wolfgang Achler

p54, by kind courtesy of Bruce Dowell

p57 (SFA022818480), Spaarnestad Photo

p59, from *Modern Motoring* magazine, June 1933 courtesy of The Richard Roberts Archive, UK

pp62-3, with kind permission from *The Caravan* magazine, UK. Photo by Andrew Paterson retouched by Adrian Harvey at the Scottish Highlander Photo Archive

Chapter 3 – France and Belgium

pp69 (btv1b531294534), 72 (bpt6k9758775h), 74 (bottom left) (bpt6k96043098), 75 (bottom right) (bpt6k6545273n), 79 (btv1b6910968t), 81 (bpt6k9605373r), 82 (top) (bpt6k65084149), 82 (bottom) (btv1b6921219h), 83 (btv1b90374406), 84 (btv1b9037441m), 85 (btv1b53052375q), 87 (top) (cb34350058s), from Bibliothèque nationale de France (Gallica), France

p70, from *La Maison à Vapeur* by Jules Verne, first published in 1880

p71, photo Fernand Révil, 1894. Collection Edith de Craene

pp73 (top and bottom), 74 (bottom right), from *La Nature* of 16 April 1898 by kind courtesy of the Conservatoire numérique des Arts et Métiers (Cnum), France

p75 (bottom left), from *Grace's Guide to British Industrial History*

p76, © Illustrated London News Ltd / Mary Evans

p77, from *The Car* magazine of 4 January 1905, courtesy of The Richard Roberts Archive, UK

p78 (REF147841), Scherl / Süddeutsche Zeitung Photo

pp80, 87 (bottom), 88, 90, 91 (top), 91 (bottom), 96 (top), 96 (bottom), 98, 99, by kind courtesy of Pierre-François Dupond

p86 (top), with kind permission from *The Caravan* magazine, UK

p86 (bottom), from *Le Camping Pratique Pour Tous* by Baudry de Saunier (Flammarion, Paris, 1937) by kind courtesy of Pierre-François Dupond

pp 89, 93 (top), 95, by kind courtesy of Gilles Fillaud

pp 92 (top) (SFA022818477), 92 (bottom) (SFA022818476), 93 (bottom) (SFA022818479), 94 (SFA022818478), Spaarnestad Photo

p97, by kind courtesy of Pierre-François Dupond and Alain Hartmann

Chapter 4 – USA

pp101 (na042687), 137 (na042673), 140 (centre left) (042683), 140 (centre middle) (na042678), 140 (centre right) (na042680), 140 (bottom left) (na042681), 140 (bottom right) (na042679), Detroit Public Library, USA

pp103 (LC-B817-7285), 104 (LC-USZ62-17356), 114 (top) (LC-B2-2261-11), 114 (bottom) (LC-B2-2261-9), 115 (left) (LC-B2-3576-3), 115 (right) (LC-B2-3576-1), 121 (top) (LC-H27-A-1071), 122 (LC-H27-A-3140), 125 (top left) (LC-F81-32197), 125 (top right) (LC-F81-39136), 125 (bottom right) (LC-F8-42451), 140 (top right) (LC-USF34-014099-E), 140 (bottom middle) (LC-USF34-019098-E), 143 (LC-USF34-009978-C), 144 (LC-USF34-002306-C), Library of Congress, Prints & Photographs Division, USA

p105 (981-695), Montana Historical Society Research Centre, USA, photo by L.A. Huffman

pp107 (YELL127596), 116 (YELL 23202, Photographer W.J. Cribbs), National Park Service, USA

p109 (top left) (*Virginia Gazette*, 6 November 1897), 109 (top right) (*Boston Daily Globe*, 20 July 1896), 109 (bottom left) (*New York Journal*, 9 May 1897), 109 (bottom right) (*Jersey City News*, 18 March 1899), from *Chronicling America: Historic American Newspapers*, Library of Congress, USA

p110 (LCCN 99001572), from *Across America in the only House on Wheels: or, Lasley's Traveling Palace* by M.E.A. Lasley, Library of Congress, USA

p111, *Automobile Topics* (USA), 18 March 1905

p112, National Motor Museum Trust, UK

pp113, 125 (bottom left), courtesy of the Pierce-Arrow Society, USA p117 (top), *Motor Magazine* (USA), December 1909

pp 117, 118 (top), 118 (bottom), courtesy of the Joel Silvey Collection at popupcamperhistory.com

pp119, 120, courtesy of the California History Room, California State Library, Sacramento, California, USA

pp121 (bottom), 124, courtesy of the Tin Can Tourists, USA

p123 (WAS0699), Special Collections, University of Washington Libraries, USA

pp 127 (top), 127 (bottom), 128, 129, 130 (top), 130 (bottom), 131, 132 (left), 132 (right), Glenn H. Curtiss Museum, Hammondsport, NY, USA

p133, McLean County Museum of History, Illinois, USA

pp 134, 135 (top right), 135 (bottom), reproduced by permission of Airstream, Inc., USA

p135 (top left), reproduced by permission of Airstream, Inc., Courtesy of the Helen Byam Schwamborn Estate, USA

pp136, 138, 140 (top left), Al Hesselbart Collection, USA

p139, courtesy of The Richard Roberts Archive, UK and LAT Images

p140 (top middle), with kind permission from *The Caravan* magazine, UK

p141 (00044861), Streib, Art./Herald Examiner Collection/Los Angeles Public Library, USA

p142, Brooks Stevens, (American, 1911-1995); Plankinton Company; Land Cruiser, 1938-06-20; 8x10 BW negative; Brooks Stevens Archive, Milwaukee Art Museum, USA, Gift of the Brooks Stevens Family and the Milwaukee Institute of Art and Design; BSA_0037; Side view; Land Cruiser

Chapter 5 – Germany

pp147, 153, 154, Dethleffs GmbH & Co. KG, Germany

p148, photo 1920 © Sammlung Siebold/Pfennig, Germany

p149 (CD_82810), Archives, Deutsches Museum, Munich, Germany

p150 (left),150 (right), © bpk-Bildagentur/Kunstbibliothek, SMB, Photothek Willy Römer/Willy Römer

p151, MAN Truck and Bus Historical Archive, Germany

p152, © bpk-Bildagentur/Hans Schaller

pp155, 156, 157, © bpk-Bildagentur

pp158, 159 (all), by kind courtesy of Hellmut Hirth

p160, © bpk-Bildagentur/Theo Rockenfeller

Chapter 6 – Australia

p163, photo by Bill Pidgeon by kind courtesy of Peter Pidgeon

pp164 (770523), 173 (774209), 175 (766546), Museums Victoria, Australia

p165 (top), from *Voyages in a Caravan* by Frank Styant Browne (Launceston Library and Brobok, 2002) p165 (bottom), from *The King's Caravan: Across Australia in a Wagon* by E.J. Brady (Edward Arnold, 1911)

pp166 (9918351240202061), 176 (bottom) (99183512940002061), 181 (99183506648802061), State Library of Queensland, Australia

p167 (top left), from the article *The Open Road – The Joys of Life in a Caravan* by Charles Barrett (1912)

pp167 (bottom right) (B54314), 169 (B59120), State Library of South Australia, Australia

p168 (top left), *The Sunday Times* 27 June 1926, courtesy of National Library of Australia/Trove

p168 (bottom right), by kind courtesy of Caren Crawford

p170, © C. Heysen, from the photo archive of The Cedars, Hahndorf, South Australia, Australia

p171 (018155PD), State Library of Western Australia, Australia

p172 (left), by kind courtesy of The National Caravan Museum, Australia and ourtouringpast.com

p172 (right), with kind permission from *The Caravan* magazine, UK

p174 (left and right), with kind permission of the Australian Childrens Theatre Foundation (ACTF), Australia

p176, by kind courtesy of Jeffry Gill

p177 (right) (110004448), State Library of NSW, Australia

pp177 (left), 178, 179, 180, from the collection of Bill Propert by kind courtesy of Michael Tierney

p182, by kind courtesy of The Sir Henry Royce Foundation and the Rolls-Royce Owners Club of Australia

p183 (110053698), Mitchell Library, State Library of New South Wales, Australia, courtesy Sam Hood

Chapter 7 – New Zealand

p185, by kind courtesy of Richard Reynolds

p186, by kind courtesy of Pauline Davis

p187 (14075578), *Otago Witness*, 10 February 1904. Alexander Turnbull Library, Wellington, New Zealand

pp188 (*Auckland Weekly News*, 6 March 1919, AWNS-19190306-40-5), 190 (top left and right) (*Auckland Weekly News*, 23 October 1924, AWNS-19241023-54-4), 195 (top) (*Auckland Weekly News*, 1 April 1936, AWNS-19360401-49-2), Auckland Libraries Heritage Collections, New Zealand

p189 (MT2011.185.262), Mataura Museum, New Zealand

p190 (bottom right), *Otago Daily Times*, 16 May 1934, courtesy of Allied Press Ltd and the National Library of New Zealand

p191 (top), *New Zealand Herald*, 9 July 1931 (p4), © NZME courtesy of the National Library of New Zealand

p191 (bottom) (PH70/3.30), Auckland War Memorial Museum, New Zealand

p192 (top left) (2019P_2013-36_026936), 192 (top right) (2019P_2013-36_026938), Palmerston North City Library, New Zealand

p192 (bottom right), *Ellesmere Guardian*, 30 April 1937, courtesy Stuff Limited and the National Library of New Zealand

p193, with kind permission from *The Caravan* magazine, UK

p194 (187810), Ellis Dudgeon Collection, Nelson Provincial Museum, New Zealand

p195 (bottom), by kind courtesy of Ted Davidson

Chapter 8 – Special Purpose Coaches, Caravans and Motorhomes

Appendix

About the Author

REFERENCES

Brunkowski J. and Closen M., *Don't Call Them Trailer Trash* (Schiffer Publishing, Atglen, 2017)

Burkhart B. and Hunt D., *Airstream: The History of the Land Yacht* (Chronicle Books, San Francisco, 2000)

Cameron L.C.R., *The Book of The Caravan* (L. Upcott Gill, London, 1909)

Constance H., *First in The Field: A Century of the Camping and Caravanning Club* (Camping and Caravanning Club, Coventry, 2001)

Culpin, Mary Shivers. 2003. "For the Benefit and Enjoyment of the People": A History of the Concession Development in Yellowstone National Park, 1872–1966. National Park Service, Yellowstone Center for Resources, Yellowstone National Park, Wyoming, YCR-CR-2003-01

Cutriss F., *Romany Life: Experienced and Observed During Many Years of Friendly Intercourse with the Gypsies* (Mills & Boon, London, 1915)

Ellesmere R., *British Caravans Volume 1: Makes founded before World War Two* (Herridge & Sons, Beaworthy, 2012)

Flanders J., *Consuming Passions: Leisure and Pleasure in Victorian Britain* (Harper Press, London, 2006)

Harmon D. L., *American camp culture: a history of recreational vehicles development and leisure camping in the United States, 1890-1960* (Iowa State University, 2001)

Harris Stone J., *Caravanning and Camping Out* (Jenkins Limited, London, 1914)

Hesselbart A., *The Dumb Things Sold – Just Like That!* (Legacy Ink Publishing, USA, 2007)

Hutchings B., *Caravanning Made Easy* (Simpkin & Company, London, 1914)

Jenkinson A., *Caravans: The Illustrated History 1919-1959* (Veloce Publishing, Dorchester, 2003)

Jenkinson A., *Motorhomes: The Illustrated History* (Veloce Publishing, Dorchester, 2003)

Jenkinson A., *The Story of Caravans International* (Amberley Publishing, Stroud, 2017)

Jessup E., *The Motor Camping Book* (G.P. Putnam's Sons, London and New York, 1921)

Keister D., *Mobile Mansions: Taking "Home Sweet Home" on the Road* (Gibbs Smith, Layton, 2006)

Keister D. and Gellner A., *Ready to Roll: The Travel Trailer in America* (Schiffer Publishing, Atglen, 2014)

Keister D., *Silver Palaces: America's Streamlined Trailers* (Gibbs Smith, Layton, 2004)

Kimball W.A. and Decker M.H., *Touring with Tent and Trailer* (Whittlesey House, New York and London, 1937)

Kubisch U., *Laube auf Rädern* (Westermann, Braunschweig, 1989)

Lanham S., *Little Book of Caravans* (G2 Entertainment, Reigate, 2011)

Montagu, Lord and Georgano G.N., *Early Days on The Road* (Michael Joseph, London, 1976)

Nash C.E., *Trailer Ahoy!* (Intelligencer Printing Company, Lancaster, 1937)

Noyes P., *Trailerama* (Gibbs Smith, Layton, 2012)

Poulin F. and Poulin É., *L'Esprit du Camping* (Editions Cheminements, France, 2005)

Robertson P., *The New Shell Book of Firsts* (Headline Book Publishing, London, 1994)

Smith B., *The Whole Art of Caravanning* (Longmans, Green and Co., London, 1907)

Stables G., *The Cruise of the Land Yacht Wanderer, Or, Thirteen Hundred Miles in my Caravan* (Hodder and Stoughton, London, 1886)

Thornburg D.A., *Galloping Bungalows: The Rise and Demise of the American House Trailer* (Shoestring Press, Connecticut, 1991)

Wallis A.D., *Wheel Estate: The Rise and Decline of Mobile Homes* (Oxford University Press, Oxford, 1991)

Whiteman W.M., *The History of The Caravan* (Blandford Press, London, 1973)

Wilson N., *Gypsies and Gentlemen* (Columbus Books, London, 1986)

Wood D.F., *RVs & Campers 1900-2000* (Iconografix, Hudson, 2002)

ABOUT THE AUTHOR

Andrew enjoyed many family caravan holidays as a child. He studied languages at Trinity College, Cambridge and then embarked on an international career in finance, property and tourism spanning six countries. He emigrated with his family to Australia in 2000 and has since held senior operational roles at the Sydney Opera House, Charles Darwin University and the Sydney Harbour Federation Trust. In his five-year search for the perfect Australian caravan, Andrew wrote *The Caravan Buyers Guide* in 2014. Now semi-retired, Andrew enjoys his two main hobbies of writing about the history of recreational vehicles and exploring the beauty of Australia by camper trailer. Andrew lives in Sydney, Australia.

For more stories and photos of early RVs, visit Andrew's website:

rvhistory.com

The author in front of *The Wanderer* (UK, 2019)

INDEX